How to Take Charge of Your Teaching Career

Also available from Continuum

9 Habits of Highly Effective Teachers, Jacquie Turnbull
Teacher's Survival Guide, Angela Thody, Barbara Gray and Derek
Bowden
The Naked Teacher, Louisa Leaman

Also by Margaret Adams

How to assess staff training and development needs in your school
The work-life balance trainer's manual
Work-life balance: a practical guide for teachers

How to Take Charge of Your Teaching Career

Margaret Adams

continuum

Continuum International Publishing Group
The Tower Building   80 Maiden Lane, Suite 704
11 York Road   New York
London   NY 10038
SE1 7NX

www.continuumbooks.com

British Library Cataloguing-in-Publication Data
A catalogue record for this book is available from the British Library.

ISBN: 9781847060310 (paperback)

Library of Congress Cataloging-in-Publication Data
A catalog record for this book is available from the Library of Congress.

Typeset by YHT Ltd, London
Printed and bound in Great Britain by Cromwell Press, Trowbridge, Wiltshire

Contents

Chapter One

Why career management matters

1.1   About this book

This is a book for every teacher.

It's a book to help you to put yourself in charge of your teaching career and by doing so to help you to have more control over every aspect of your life. It's a book to help you to understand where you are in your career today and to decide where you want to be, in the future. More importantly, this is a book that will help you to get there.

1.2   Why you need this book

Teaching careers are shaped by the decisions teachers make – or fail to make – about their working lives. During your career you will make decisions about what you want from your work again and again. These decisions are important. Your decisions will affect how you spend your time at work and how satisfied you are with your working life. They will affect whether you decide to stay in your current job or move on. They will affect how much you earn, which, in turn, will affect what you can do with your life outside work. Your decisions will even affect your retirement years, because you will be shaping your retirement income when you make your decisions about your career and your working life.

Yet most people don't give much consideration to their careers, and in this teachers are no different from the rest of the population. Lots of teachers only think about their careers when:

- they are considering applying for another job
- the management system in their school forces them to do so
- a crisis occurs in their lives.

Even in these circumstances many teachers only think superficially about their careers.

They may think about a job opportunity that has presented itself, but often do not consider where this particular job fits into their whole career, and if it helps them to fulfil their long-term plans for their career.

The management system in school may oblige teachers to give some thought to their careers when the annual review or appraisal comes around. Yet, teachers are often reluctant to reflect on their careers, especially if they know they have not done as much as they might to control and direct them, or they think they have limited options for pursuing the sort of career they want.

Many teachers only think seriously about their careers when a crisis looms. Sometimes the crisis occurs when teachers realize they are unhappy in their roles and they look around for a new job. At that time they often focus more attention on getting out of their current situation than on getting into a better one. Sometimes something unexpected happens in a teacher's life. It might be serious illness that forces a re-examination of priorities. It might be the break-up of a relationship. When a crisis occurs those teachers who have given little thought to their careers often have no choice but to make far-reaching decisions about their futures in stressful circumstances.

Lots of teachers just drift from year to year. Some teachers say they don't have a career to think about. Some teachers say they're too old for a career, or too new to the profession to think about a career, or maybe they say they are just passing through teaching on their way to something else.

In fact most people spend more time planning their annual holiday than they spend thinking about their careers.

And if I've just described the way you manage – or fail to manage – your career, then that's what you need to change.

Wherever you are in your teaching career, whether you are old or young, in a leadership role or spending all your time in a classroom, you need to think about how the decisions you make about your career are going to affect your life in teaching now and in the future. You need to think about these decisions in a systematic and circumspect way.

1.3 Decision points in a teaching career

Teachers everywhere are faced with the same sorts of decisions and challenges when they think about managing their careers. It doesn't matter where you teach, or how the education system is organized where you work, you will reach points in your career when you will be faced with making decisions about what to do next.

This book will help you to make the decisions that are right for you when you reach those points in your career, by asking you to consider the main questions you really must answer when you're:

- deciding how you wish to develop your career
- deciding if or when to change schools
- deciding if or when to seek promotion
- deciding whether or not to downshift
- deciding when to leave the profession.

Remember that asking yourself the right questions at the right time is one of the most important aspects of career management. Yes, some of the questions are difficult, and some of the questions are ones you would rather not think about, but your success in managing your career will depend on how committed you are to finding answers to those difficult questions.

Using this book will help you to do that, because this book is a personal guide and reference book. Read it now, but keep it handy for as long as you remain in teaching. You'll need to refer to it more than once!

1.4   Does this sound like you?

Even though you know this all makes sense, perhaps you'd still rather not think seriously about your career. Maybe you've promised yourself that you'll think about it later, when things have settled down in your life, when you've more time, when there aren't so many other pressing things to think about.

Well, you know this is just prevarication. You also know how to deal with those objections. Teachers are clever people. Most teachers know they should give some thought to their careers on a regular basis and often criticize themselves for not doing so, but, as you probably know, teachers everywhere find lots of reasons to avoid this task.

If that sounds like you, look at the questions below. Could you imagine yourself saying any of these things? If you could, then you know it's time for you to rethink your approach to your career.

I only think about my career when it's time for my review/appraisal.
If you say this, then you know you're drifting. You know you need to think about your career more than once a year, because you really can't be sure you're making the best decisions if you make them at a time chosen by someone else and devote only minimal attention to the activity.

I don't have time to think about my career.
Your career is going to affect everything about your life, your prospects, your income, your relationships, your retirement. So, ask yourself what could be more important than planning the shape of your working life. You know that – if you want to – you will find time for something as important as reviewing your career.

I don't have a career. Teaching's just a job.
You are making decisions about your working life all the time. Those decisions are shaping your life. This means you have a career. Your decisions today and tomorrow build on all the decisions you have made to date. Maybe you're not aware of how you are directing our career. If you say you don't have a career, perhaps you're just not thinking about the everyday decisions you make as part of a larger plan.

I'm not looking for promotion, so why do I need to think about my career?
It's one of the most damaging career myths around to think that because you don't want to get to the top, you don't have a career. You have a course to plot, a journey to make and a map to draw. Every one does, so you, like every one else, should think about your career. Plan that journey to make sure you end up at a destination which suits you.

I'm too old to have a career.
The best way to close down opportunities at any point in your career is to think negatively about yourself. It doesn't have to be age that gets in the way. It could be anything: the wrong qualifications, or the lack of qualifications, the lack of experience in a particular field, or at a particular level and so on. You'll find it much easier to plan and manage your career if you start thinking about what you can do and what you can contribute, rather than creating barriers and offering reasons why you can't succeed, and shouldn't be allowed to succeed, at something new, however old you are.

There aren't any opportunities for advancement, so why should I bother?
You never know what's out there, and anyway one of the things successful people say again and again is that part of their success comes from being ready to seize an opportunity when it presents itself, or when they go looking for it. If you make sure you are ready to jump when the time is right, you won't miss the opportunities there are. Once you are

alert and looking for opportunities you might find there are more of them out there than you thought.

I hate teaching. I'd leave if only there was something else I could do. Being unhappy with what you do on a day-to-day basis is never a good situation in which to find yourself. If you are truly unhappy, then you need to start thinking seriously about your career immediately. You need to look at roles in teaching and beyond and decide on the direction in which you intend to travel. However, the longer you have been in teaching, the more carefully you should think about a career move out of the profession. You will need to take professional advice on such issues as pensions and retirement planning before you make your move.

One thing is certain, if you are unhappy with your working life, then you do need to rethink your approach to managing your career, because what you're doing right now isn't working.

1.5   The format of the book

This is a book of questions and answers. The Q & A format is becoming increasingly popular as a means of helping people to learn.

The Q & A format is a very user-friendly and user-orientated way of working and one which most of us, because we are internet users, find easy to use. We are used to reading FAQs (frequently asked questions) online and using them to help us to understand complex and unfamiliar subjects without calling on the support of others. The questions and answers in this book are, in fact, FAQs about career management.

The Q & A format is also a learner-centred way of working. It deals with issues in ways which have relevance to the people asking the questions, and in ways which make sense to them. This format will also help you to learn quickly. If you want answers to questions, you do not need to read the whole book or even a complete chapter, you can simply work through the list of questions and find the ones which most readily fit your concerns.

In order to make the questions and answers in this book relevant, I have drawn on my experience of working in staff development in education and on the work I undertake with teachers and lecturers as an HR consultant, helping them to manage their careers more effectively and helping them to put themselves in control of their lives. I know, therefore, that the questions and answers in this book are exactly the types of questions that people in education who are thinking seriously about their careers ask. The answers here *are* relevant to people working in education today.

1.6   How the book is organized

This book is divided into seven further chapters. Each chapter covers a different career management issue. These are the main issues you will need to deal with when you reach the important decision points in your teaching career.

The introduction to each chapter gives you an overview of what is covered and when that chapter is likely to be most useful to you. Questions linked to each chapter's theme, and asked from the perspective of a teacher dealing with the issues raised in the chapter, follow the introduction. They are the sort of questions you would be likely to ask yourself if you were trying to come to a decision about that particular career issue. This makes the content of each chapter relevant to you, the reader.

Chapter Two is about career planning. This chapter will help you to put your career on the right development track. It will help you to understand why planning is important and how to define your career aspirations and career goals. **Chapter Three** is for teachers at the beginning of their careers and for those taking on new roles. This chapter will help you to define a range of survival strategies, set your career on the right course and begin to be aware of what you do well as a teacher.

Chapter Four is about developing your career. It will help you to be clear about what is important in your working life and to shape your career to ensure you are taking it in a direction that will help you to have a meaningful, satisfying and fulfilling life as a teacher.

Chapter Five is for teachers who have decided they wish to pursue promotion and advancement within teaching. It will help you to be clear on how far you wish to progress your career, along with the major development options available to you. It will help you to decide if you wish to become a head teacher. It also offers some advice on what to do if you think you have made some career management mistakes.

Chapter Six will help teachers to reassess their current career management strategies. Doing this will help you to decide if you want to change career direction, and to identify the right career choices for you. It will help you to decide what to do if you *don't* want promotion, if you *do* want to take on a post with less responsibility or if you want to review your whole approach to career management.

Chapter Seven deals with the issues teachers face then they are seriously considering leaving teaching, whether they are leaving to retire or to take up career options outside teaching. This chapter will help you to ensure that you review the key issues before making the major change to your career management strategy that leaving teaching would necessitate.

Chapter Eight draws together all the themes and issues raised throughout the book to help you to create a relevant and flexible career management strategy and to help you to develop the expertise you need to manage your career well.

There is a summary at the end of each chapter which allows you to review the chapter's content quickly.

There are also activities based on the major themes and issues at the end of each chapter. You are encouraged to write down your responses to the questions asked in the activities and use this information to help you to produce, or review, your career management plan when you work through Chapter Eight. Your notes will also help you to complete each stage of the career planning process and to decide what to do in particular circumstances, whether or not you also create an overall career management plan.

1.7   How to use the book

You can use the book in any way that matches your needs and your preferences. You can dip in and out of the chapters in whatever way suits you. Flicking through the book, and finding the parts that are most relevant to your situation today, is probably the best way to familiarize yourself with the book's approach.

Refer to the different chapters in the order that seems right for you. There is no need to read the chapters sequentially. If you turn to the chapter that is most relevant to your current situation, you will find questions that teachers considering the same issues that you are thinking about are likely to be asking.

Use the introduction to each chapter to help you to decide how relevant the contents are to your situation. Then work through the questions, always thinking how best to apply the guidance to your circumstances.

However, you should remember that your circumstances are unique and this book can only offer general advice about how to deal with your personal career choices. It's up to you to decide how relevant the guidance is to your own situation. It's up to you to find advisers and guides who will be familiar enough with your own career and your aspirations to offer you personalized support.

At some point you are strongly recommended to make a commitment to yourself to think about your career in a focused but unhurried way. At this point, try to find time to read Chapter Two: Planning your career, and Chapter Four: Developing your career, in depth. Working through these chapters will help you to make better use of the rest of the book.

When you become more confident that you are beginning to take charge of your career, use Chapter Eight to help you to produce a career management plan.

Summary

1. This book is for all teachers.
2. Most teachers don't give enough consideration to how they manage their careers, often thinking about them only when they are considering applying for another job, preparing for their appraisal or when faced with a crisis in their personal or professional lives.
3. Every teacher has a career which needs to be managed. This is true whether or not teachers are looking for promotion, wherever they are in their careers and whatever their age.
4. This book will help teachers when they are thinking about how to survive the early weeks and months in teaching, how to progress their careers, whether they wish to become head teachers, when they want to change direction and when they are thinking of leaving teaching.
5. The book's format and layout will help teachers to find the sections which are most relevant to their situations easily.

Activity – Looking ahead

Overview

This activity will help you to look carefully at what you want to achieve in your career in the next few years.

Task

You are going to write down your most important career achievements over the last three years as if you were producing the information for your diary or for your blog.

When you come to write your entry – or series of entries – you will make it clear:

- the range of activities you currently undertake
- what you do on a typical working day
- what aspects of your work you really like
- the reasons why you do this job
- what you think you do well.

An easy task? Maybe.

1. Before you begin writing take today's date and add three years to it. Put this date at the top of your sheet of paper or on the top line of your computer screen. Then write the diary entries or blogs as if you were writing them three years from now, and as if you had fulfilled your current plans for your career.
2. Take your time. Put in as much detail as you think necessary to enable you to see a full picture of your work.
3. Now think of three things you intend to do to make the account you have just written real. Write them down. One of these activities should be something you could do in the next three months.
4. When you have finished the task note a date when you will return to the activity to review your progress towards fulfilling your aspirations.
5. Keep your notes safe. You will need to refer to them again later, when you come to produce your career management plan.

Refer to the notes you have made when completing these activities whenever you are thinking about your career aspirations and your career goals.

Chapter Two

Planning your career

2.1   Overview

This chapter is for teachers starting to plan their careers.

It sets out a series of questions you are likely to ask yourself when you begin your career planning process.

This chapter will help you to:

- develop a better understanding of what a career in teaching means to you
- understand what motivates you as teacher
- decide how far ahead you can realistically plan your career
- begin to plan your teaching career.

Use the questions in this chapter whenever you want to take stock and to think carefully about your life in teaching, especially if you have never undertaken any serious careering planning activities before.

Use this chapter before you make any far-reaching career choices, and again once you have settled into a new situation or role. Use it whenever you are thinking about a career change, for example, seeking a promotion, a change of school or a sideways move into another area of teaching. Use it also when you are preparing for your performance review or appraisal.

Use it whenever you think the time is right for you to give some serious consideration to where you are taking your career.

Use this chapter in conjunction with Chapter Four, which is about developing your career, and Chapter Eight, which deals with how best to bring all the components of the career planning process together.

The chapter is divided into three further parts:

- why career planning matters
- understanding yourself
- career planning basics.

You will find questions you might ask yourself about the different stages of career planning as you work through these sections. Consider how relevant the answers offered to the questions are to your own circumstances. Then complete the activities at the end of the chapter.

2.2   Why career planning matters

When you commit to career planning you are taking the first step towards taking charge of your teaching career. Most people accept that planning is a good thing, but often just don't do it. This can mean they don't plan their careers or their lives outside work. Yet planning is the basic component of career management; you need to master it.

Planning is time-consuming and difficult. Is it really necessary?
Yes, it is, and you probably know why.

Just about every one knows some good advice about planning. Teachers will often tell their classes that failing to plan is planning to fail, or that proper planning prevents poor performance. It's also worth considering how you can judge your success – however you choose to measure it – if you don't know where you are going. And, of course, ask yourself the question, if you don't know where you're going, does it really matter where you end up?

If you don't plan your career, you are either drifting or you are allowing someone else to direct your career for you. As a result you might end up in some interesting places. Then again, you might end up somewhere dreadful. It's all a matter of luck. While you are drifting no one has any control over your journey, or where it is taking you. On the other hand, while someone else is directing you, and your career, you are acting in line with another person's values, aspirations and beliefs rather than your own.

Neither course of action is desirable. If you want to be in charge of your journey, and of your career, you need to plan for yourself.

What is a career anyway?
In this book the term 'career' is used to define a teacher's whole working life. If you use this definition, then every one has a career. Confusion arises because people often define their careers in very different ways. There's nothing wrong with that, but you need to be sure you understand what you mean when you talk about your career.

Is there a generally accepted definition of what a career actually is?
There are lots of definitions and new ones are emerging all the time as working life changes, and as people's expectations of their working lives change. This means there is no single, universally accepted description of a career, so the concept of generally accepted definitions really doesn't enter into things.

To help you to arrive at a definition with which you will be comfortable, it's probably helpful to think about the some of the terms teachers use when describing their work. The four most commonly used terms are:

1. **Career** – often defined as a course or progress through life and/or working life and sometimes considered in terms of advancing oneself in one's area of work.
2. **Job** – usually defined as a paid position of employment and sometimes used in a derogatory sense: 'It's just a job.'
3. **Profession** – a role that is often linked with advanced learning such as law or medicine, where the role holders gain some additional status because of their membership of an exclusive group.

4. **Vocation** – this is, quite literally, a calling, meaning a particular trade or profession to which someone is particularly well suited. Someone with a vocation wishes to commit totally to that role.

If you accept the above definitions of these terms, you will see that a person is likely to have a range of jobs in the course of a career. Collectively the jobs a teacher holds during his or her working life add up to a career. Teaching is usually defined as a profession, and most people in teaching consider themselves to be professionals, whether they are thinking about their current job or their career. A teacher who is passionately committed to the job can have a vocation for teaching while working as a professional in a particular job and pursuing a defined career path.

You need to be clear about how you define your work as a teacher because this will shape your beliefs about your career options and how you manage your teaching life.

This isn't the way I have heard careers described in the past, so are these other definitions wrong?
No.

In order to avoid misunderstanding, when you talk to people about the concept of a career, you will need to remember that other people may define a teaching career differently from the way you define it. This is inevitable because the meanings people give to the term 'career' and to the concept of the career are changing.

Things get confused because for many years people thought about careers in terms of seeking promotion, getting a better job and earning more money. You had a career if you were doing these things. Climbing the ladder is still a widely used metaphor for making progress in a career. Those who are not climbing the ladder, or those who have got as far up the career ladder as they are able to climb, are, in some circles, still judged to be somehow less worthy and less successful than those who have pushed on to the topmost rungs. This concept of a career probably led to the belief that those who are not actively trying to get to the top of the ladder do not have a career.

You need to ensure that while you are aware of the different ways in which people define careers, you should still work out your own definition of a teaching career and what you think about your role as a teacher.

I've got a definition of my career that I'm happy to work with, so do I start to think about the jobs I would like to aim for?
No, not yet.

Take a step back and focus on yourself first. You need to understand yourself before you can begin to plan your career. You need to understand what is important to you in terms of your work before you do any serious career planning. Therefore, give some thought to your personality and what motivates you at work, before you start work on your career management plan. This will take time but only you can do it.

2.3   Understanding yourself

If you rely on other people to tell you what's important in your career, and where you should be travelling on your career journey, you will inevitably be influenced by their judgements and feelings about careers and career paths. Their ideas will not necessarily fit your circumstances. Their lives are different from yours. They will inevitably want different things from their careers from what will be right for you. Sooner or later, following *their* desires will almost certainly take you in the wrong direction.

You need to find out what's important to you, what motivates you and what will give you satisfaction in your career to enable you to start your own career planning activities.

I don't really know what's important to me. What can I do to get started?
The best way to begin to think about this is to think about what motivates you.

Motivation is all about the relationship between what you're trying to reach, the places you want to arrive at, and what you're trying to avoid, or the places you want to get away from. Sometimes, during your teaching career, you will actively be heading towards a goal you have defined: a promotion, a specialism, etc. Sometimes you will be trying to get away from something or someone: the job you no longer enjoy, the new head teacher, the difficult head of department.

It's always better to be making changes in your life for positive reasons, that is moving towards a goal, rather than simply moving away from a problem. You've probably heard the expression: 'Out of the frying pan, into the fire.' That's what can happen if your attention is on getting out of a difficult situation without giving the right amount of thought to where you are going.

How do I work out what motivates me as a teacher?
When most teachers think about motivation they think about one or more of the following:

- rewards
- recognition
- personal development and learning
- helping others.

You should think about all four and check out which are more important to you than the others.

With rewards, for example, most people think first about financial rewards. If reward is the most important motivating force for you, you will seek out roles that offer the highest salaries. This will almost inevitably mean you will seek promotion and advancement in teaching. If financial reward is important to you, then being a subject teacher or a class teacher will not be enough for you. You will want to earn more than these grades of teacher earn.

Sometimes people who are looking for reward focus on status and view status as their reward, rather than income. They may seek out roles that give them authority over others or enhanced freedom of action to enable them to introduce new ideas and new ways of working in school.

Most people who value reward highly think regularly in terms of comparisons. They are very aware of salary differentials and hierarchies and their place in them. They are regularly measuring themselves against others, especially in terms of earnings or status. They are often highly competitive. They are likely to define their successes in terms of their achievements in relation to the achievements of others.

When it comes to recognition, most people who value this are looking for a very particular type of status. This is usually the status of an expert or authority. If recognition is the most important motivating force for you, you will not define your status with reference to your position in an educational hierarchy. The status you will value will come from people's respect for your achievements, your experience and the work you do. You may also have to gain the more conventional sort of status – that linked to progression in the educational hierarchy – to achieve the recognition you are looking for.

In some cases you will find yourself in the same roles as those who value reward highly. However, you will have chosen these roles because you want your contribution to be recognized and because you believe you can gain most recognition by taking on roles that also carry formal responsibility.

If personal development and learning motivate you most, your challenges are personal challenges. You want to learn, develop and grow. You probably choose roles in teaching because they require you to learn new things all the time and to take on new, and unfamiliar, tasks. It is the development opportunity linked to a new role that you relish most. When you are wrestling with challenges, you achieve most job satisfaction.

Once you have overcome difficulties you are ready to move on, to learn more and to pit yourself against a new problem. You actively dislike roles where you can do your work easily because these roles offer you insufficient challenge. It is likely that you will feel dissatisfaction with your career when you are in such a situation. Therefore, unless the roles you take on are constantly changing, you will probably want to change your job regularly, without necessarily seeking promotion.

If helping others is your key motivator, your focus will usually be on your learners, although sometimes your desire to help may be focused on helping your colleagues or on helping your school within its local community. Every teacher will claim to have learners' needs at the centre of their concerns, but for you your desire to help people is stronger than any desire you might have for promotion, increased income, personal development or recognition within your profession. This makes a difference to how you define your career and how you manage it.

As a consequence, you will seek out roles which allow you to maintain contact with learners or to take on responsibilities for developing teachers or others who work in the educational environment. If you take on additional responsibilities, you may seek out pastoral roles, or roles in which you act as a guide to teachers and to other people who work in school.

It's not as simple as that. I'm motivated by more than one thing. What does that mean for my career planning?
You are not alone. Most teachers will be motivated by more than one of the above. It's also true that their preferences and interests change over time, so what motivates them changes, too.

If you are going to have a satisfying and fulfilling life as a teacher, you will need to be sure you know which is the most important motivator at a particular point in your career. If you don't, you could find yourself taking on roles that you do not value or enjoy, but think you should, and roles in which you find your achievements are just never very satisfying. The result is disappointment and frustration for you, even if, in the eyes of others, you are a remarkable success.

You can almost certainly see the consequences of some of these poor choices around you. After a number of years in teaching some teachers become disillusioned and disenchanted with their work. This is often because they have pursued the wrong goals, possibly by seeking promotion, when perhaps they would value opportunities to focus on their learning and development more. Perhaps they have accepted a role that takes them out of the classroom in order to earn more, when they would prefer to continue to work closely with learners.

You are more likely to avoid these disappointments if you understand what motivates you, and what gives you a sense of satisfaction and fulfilment in your work. So, take the time to think carefully about motivation – now.

Should I also think about what motivates me in my life outside work?
Yes, you should.

Motivation is important in all areas of life. You will be more satisfied with your life if you are aware of the key motivators in your life beyond teaching, too.

Once I've done that, am I ready to start to think about where I want to take my career?
If you are reasonably confident you understand your own motivations, then, yes, you can start to think about your career aspirations and career goals. However, it's still too early to think about specific jobs.

2.4   Career planning basics

Now you understand your motivation and hence you have a sense of what is important to you right now, you have already begun to plan your career. You have, in fact, created a development context and rationale for all the career planning activities you will undertake as you work through this book.

Next, it is important to think about your career as a journey and remember that every journey starts with a destination in mind. This is where career goals become important. However, you also need to know why you are setting out on your journey, and why that journey is important to you. That is where career aspirations figure in your planning process.

Career goals and career aspirations. What are they, and what's the difference between them?
Your career aspirations underpin everything about your career. Your career aspirations are what you want in the long term from your career. Your career aspirations are relevant to your whole career – as far ahead as you can plan. The entire journey you intend making to fulfil your aspiration may not be clear to you now, although you will be able to see the first few steps along the way.

For example, if, as a new teacher, you aspire to become a head teacher, you will know you need to seek out positions with additional responsibilities, and responsibilities linked to leadership roles, but at the beginning of your career, the exact route to headship will almost certainly be unclear.

Alternatively, you may decide you want, above everything else, to become a recognized expert in behaviour management. This could be your lifelong ambition and the aspiration which motivates you throughout your career. When you first articulate that aspiration, you may not know what career goals you should set to help you to succeed, but your aspiration is clear.

When you come to think about how you will fulfil this career aspiration, you may decide that the next two steps on your journey are for you to gain a particular qualification and to take on a pastoral responsibility in your school, or, if one does not exist in your current school, to take a pastoral role in another school. These are your career goals, the specific destinations at which you wish to arrive as you progress through your career and work to fulfil your aspirations.

Your career goals shape your career now and in the near future. Your goals may be on your horizon, but they are not beyond it. You might have a goal to take up a particular type of responsibility in the near future or to learn a specific approach to your teaching this year or next.

I'm really struggling with this. Some people know where they want to take their careers. I don't. Does this mean I can't plan my career?
No, it just means there is another step in the process for you. You should complete this before you start to think seriously about your career aspirations and career goals.

Think about the activities you would like to do in your ideal working day. This may mean deciding which parts of your current job you like best. It may mean thinking about tasks that you would like to be part of your job, but which you do not do at present.

Next look around you. Find out who actually does the sort of work you believe will give you satisfaction. Look for the roles that will allow you to spend most of your time doing the tasks that you have identified as being the ones you find most enjoyable, satisfying and fulfilling. Talk to the people who hold these roles. Find out about their career journeys, but also find out if the detail of the jobs they are doing is what you had expected. These investigations will guide you towards the roles and responsibilities you should seek out and away from those you decide will not be suitable for you.

Once you have worked out what you want to do, and which roles will allow you to do these things, you can focus on some short-term career goals. For example, identifying the right role for you to seek out, succeeding in getting appointed to that role and then making a success of the job you take on.

This approach will help you in the present. You can then start to think about a longer-term plan, some further career goals and your career aspirations.

How far ahead does this mean I should plan when I am thinking about my career goals?
Think ahead as far as is practicable but do not try to plan your entire working life now.

Remember that people don't stay in the same careers for thirty years or more in anything like the numbers that they once did. Therefore, it doesn't make sense to plan your career as if you are going to be in teaching until you retire. Looking five years into the future is probably about as far ahead as it is reasonable to plan, and that is as far into the future as your planning horizon should be – unless, of course, you are absolutely sure of what you want to do. Even then it's worth remaining pragmatic about the more distant future.

Therefore, when you are starting to plan your career, you can safely look two career moves ahead. That is, you can think about the job you would like to do next, and the one after that. Alternatively, you can think in terms of where you would like to be in your career in three to five years' time.

That's all very well, but so much happens that is unexpected in life, is it really worth spending all this time on thinking about career goals and aspirations?
In the end it is your decision how much time you choose to give to career planning and how you use your plan.

Think about any plan you have ever made. You already know things can get in the way of its completion and push you off course. When this happens, if you know where you want to get to, you can rework your plan to help you to arrive at your defined destination. If you know where you want to go, when you are blown off course, you can travel to where you want to be using a different route from the one you originally planned. Instead of taking the train, you can choose to drive or take a bus. If you don't have a plan, then when you get buffeted, you may drift and end up somewhere unexpected, somewhere you hadn't expected to land. It's all a matter of luck as to whether this is a good or a bad destination for you.

You will need to think about how you want your life to progress. Which way do you prefer to work? What you decide is best is the right choice for you.

What happens if I want to change my career goals?
There is a good chance that you will want to change your

mind about your career goals – and possibly about your aspirations, too – at some point in your career.

Flexibility in planning is always important. The single, most important quality of your career planning process must be its flexibility. It's a fact of life that what we want in life, and what's important to us, changes. As a teacher you are no different from anyone else. What you want at one stage of your career may not be what you want later. Your aspirations will change as your experience of teaching deepens. What you decided to work towards at one point in your life will be superseded by a different aspiration later.

The world around you will also change. Opportunities which are available now may not be there in a few years' time and new opportunities will develop. If you are too rigid with your plans you may find you are forcing yourself towards goals which no longer have any value to you, or missing opportunities to do the work that you will find most fulfilling, if you allowed yourself to consider it.

So the most important message about all aspects of career planning is to make sure you have goals but to be willing to modify them when it becomes clear to you that fulfilling them is no longer taking you towards a destination you believe is right for you.

I've got my aspirations and my goals, so can I think about the jobs I want to do?

If you know what the people doing the jobs you are thinking about actually do, and that taking on these jobs will help you to achieve your career goals, then, yes.

However, you would be well advised to think about the career planning process in a little more depth before you take that step. You now have career aspirations and career goals, but you don't have an action plan, as yet. Nor do you have an implementation strategy.

Unless you are absolutely sure a job you are thinking about is right for you, continue working in the career planning process.

Remain flexible and alert, too. Keep looking at what people in different roles do. You might find different activities that interest you or different ways of achieving your goals. Think about any other roles you might choose to take on as a result of the experience you are gaining. Check them out.

Keep your career aspirations and your career goals in mind, but also keep as many options available to you as possible. Ensure that you remain aware of what motivates you and what gives you satisfaction in your work as you now move on to the next stage in career planning.

So what comes next in career planning?
If you have defined your career aspirations and you now have some career goals which you know are right for you, you have made a good start on the career planning process.

You now need to think about formulating an action plan and planning your journey towards the destinations you have identified. There's more about those activities in Chapter Four. In Chapter Eight you will learn how to put all the elements together to create a career management plan.

Keep going. You have made a good start.

Summary

1. This chapter will help teachers to begin to plan their careers and to understand why career planning is important.
2. It can be used by teachers at any point in their careers.
3. The chapter explores the concept of a career in teaching and helps teachers to arrive at an understanding of what a career is, and what it can be.
4. Before teachers can begin to plan their careers effectively they need to understand what motivates them. This will mean establishing if they primarily seek rewards, recognition, personal learning and development or to help others.
5. Teachers need career aspirations and career goals. Career aspirations underpin a teacher's career and

define what a teacher wants from his or her career in the long term. Career goals are specific destinations at which a teacher wants to arrive and are often specified in terms of jobs and responsibilities that a teacher seeks.

6. Flexibility in career planning is important as individuals' aspirations, and their personal circumstances, change. Unexpected events can also impact upon teachers' plans.

7. Once a teacher has established sound career aspirations and relevant career goals, he or she can begin to think about other planning activities and producing a career management plan.

Activities

There are two activities linked to the content of this chapter. Completing them will help you to understand yourself a little better, to be clear about your career aspirations and to formulate your career goals. The first activity is about what motivates you as a teacher. The second will help you with the career planning basics dealt with in this chapter.

Activity one – Motivation and you

Overview

This activity focuses on what is important to you as a teacher and what you are striving to achieve in your career.

Task

1. Consider the following questions and note your responses on a piece of paper. Ensure you offer at least two responses to each question. If you would like to add more answers to any of the questions, you may do so.

A   What sort of rewards do I want as a teacher?
(Rewards can be tangible, for example, salary or gaining a senior role, or intangible, for example, personal satisfaction at a job well done.)

B   What sort of recognition do I want as a teacher?
(Recognition could be offered in the form of status, for example, the status of an expert in a particular aspect of education, e.g. behaviour management or assessment, or in the value placed on your contribution in school by others.)

C   What sort of personal learning and development do I want to undertake as a teacher?
(This may take the form of qualifications or new skills or on-the-job learning. It may mean taking on new roles that require you to learn new skills.)

D   How do I want to help others in my role as a teacher?
(This could focus on helping your learners to achieve more. It might mean helping your learners to overcome difficulties which affect their ability to learn. It may mean helping other teachers and other staff in school or helping to support the local community.)

2. Look again at all your responses to questions A, B, C and D. Assume that over the next two years you can make only two of your statements become reality. Which two would you choose?
3. Now write down what you would find satisfying if you made these developments to your career.
4. Why will success with these two activities be more satisfying than achieving any of the other potential achievements you have nominated? Note down your responses and keep your answers safe.

Activity two – Career aspirations and career goals

Overview

This activity deals with formulating career aspirations and career goals. It is in three parts. The first two parts deal with helping others to define their career aspirations and career goals. The final part deals with your own career aspirations and career goals.

Task

Part one – Jazz's goals

Jazz is a teacher with three years' experience. She teaches English and enjoys teaching learners aged thirteen to sixteen best. She aspires to become a head of department in a large school with responsibility for English and associated subjects, for example, teaching English as a second language and drama. She has thought about how she is going to fulfil her aspiration, but is stuck when it comes to setting her career goals.

Assume you are working with Jazz and helping her to establish career goals – that is, agreeing specific destinations on her career development journey. Make notes in answer to the following questions and keep your responses safe.

1. How many moves do you think it will take Jazz to gain a post where she holds the type of responsibility she is looking for?
2. What sort of roles and responsibilities do you think will take Jazz to her chosen career destination?
3. What sort of career goals should Jazz set for herself for the next two years and for the next five years?

Part two – Sam's aspirations

Sam has been teaching for a year and a half and hasn't given career aspirations and career goals a thought. Sam is a class teacher working with eight and nine year olds.

Sam enjoys being in the classroom and helping young people learn. However, Sam is worried that in the future being a classroom teacher might not be sufficiently stimulating or rewarding. Sam is also worried about becoming disillusioned with teaching and is having trouble planning for the future.

1. Assume you are working with Sam and want to help this teacher to establish some career aspirations. As part of this process you ask Sam the following questions:

    - Which part of your job do you enjoy the most?
    - On which parts of your job would you like to spend more time?
    - What sort of roles exist in school that allow teachers to spend more of their time on the tasks that you enjoy?
    - How might you gain one of these roles?
    - How long do you think it would take you to gain such a role?
    - Would you be happy if you held that type of responsibility?

As you work with Sam, you discover that this teacher loves music and has a good singing voice. You also discover that Sam has a flair for design which is not being used to any great extent at present.

2. What sort of career aspirations – that is, long-term plans – could this discussion help Sam to establish? Write down your responses and keep your notes safe.

Part three – your own career aspirations and goals
Use this part of the activity to help you with your own career aspirations and career goals. If you have already formulated those aspirations and goals, use the activity to confirm you are happy with your decisions. Make a note of your responses to all the questions and keep your notes safe.

1. Read through the following statements and on a separate sheet of paper use your own career aspirations to complete as many of the statements as you can.

    a. I want to be recognized as an expert in ... *(nominate an area of teaching and learning or a related aspect of education).*

    b. I want to spend my time in teaching helping people to ... *(describe the work you want to undertake with people – and specify which people, e.g. learners).*

    c. I want to gain the status of ... *(nominate a role or a specialist status).*

    d. I want to be rewarded at the level of ... *(nominate a role, a salary level or some other tangible return for your inputs).*

2. Which of the career aspirations which you have nominated would you most like to achieve? Order the statements, noting which ones you wish to achieve most.

3. What sort of roles will you need to hold in the next two years in order to move closer to fulfilling the career aspirations you have just defined?

4. What sort of roles will you need to hold in the next five years in order to move you closer to fulfilling your career aspirations?

5. What roles do you think you will need to hold in the more distant future in order to enable you to fulfil your career aspirations?

6. How many moves do you think it will take you to find yourself in a position where you hold the type of responsibility you want?

Notes about Jazz and Sam

Ensure Jazz checks out the careers of two or three heads of department before deciding how long it is going to take her to reach her goals. She needs to know how careers develop and progress and gain some insights into how she might best manage her own career before she can formalize her plan.

Helping Sam will entail reviewing where he or she is going in terms of a career in teaching. You will need to encourage Sam to map out the possibilities, including those linked to the musical interests and those linked to design. Deciding what to do next is then Sam's choice.

Refer to the notes you have made when completing these activities whenever you are thinking about your career aspirations and your career goals.

Chapter Three

Starting your career

3.1 Overview

This chapter is for teachers at the beginning of their careers who want to manage their early years at work, and especially that important first year as a teacher, positively and successfully.

It offers newly qualified teachers and beginning teachers guidance on how to use their initial experiences in school to start to shape their careers in ways that will help them to succeed in their chosen profession.

Those returning to teaching after a break, and more experienced teachers taking on new roles and responsibilities, may also find this chapter useful as they work to manage their transition from one role to another.

Use this chapter to put your career on the right track from your very first days as a teacher or in a new teaching role.

The chapter is divided into three further parts:

- starting out in teaching
- survival strategies
- finding your very special talents.

You will find questions you might ask yourself about managing your early weeks and months in teaching, or in a new role, in each section. Review the answers and judge how relevant they are to your situation. Then complete the activities at the end of the chapter.

3.2   Starting out in teaching

At the beginning of your teaching career comes induction. Wherever you begin teaching you will have an induction of one sort or another. When you take on a new role, or return to teaching after a break, you should also expect to receive an induction.

Every one seems to pay a lot of attention to induction and the induction process. Why is that?
Most schools expend a lot of effort helping new teachers to settle into the job of being a teacher.

The first weeks and months in the job are an important time in every teacher's career. This is the time when the school and new teacher begin to work towards a decision as to whether teaching is the right career for that individual and to establish what support the new teacher needs to enable him or her to be as successful as possible.

However, there's a lot of misunderstanding about induction. Induction has a single purpose. That is to enable you to cope with the job you have taken on. For that reason alone it is very important. Only when you can function in your role without extra support should you consider your induction has ended. That's where the misunderstanding comes into things. Most new teachers think their induction has finished long before it really has.

Those who are responsible for helping new teachers to adjust to the demands of the profession know that levels of teacher wastage are higher in the first three to five years of teaching than in subsequent years. This is a trend that is found in the majority of occupations. Most labour turnover occurs among new employees. Therefore, many schools do their best to make sure new teachers stay by giving them a good induction.

The same rules about induction apply when an experienced teacher takes on a new role. The purpose of the induction process is to help him or her to learn how to cope with the demands of the job quickly.

What should I expect of my induction?
Your induction should help you to make the transition from new worker to competent worker.

Your induction begins when you accept that first teaching job. Induction will help you through the first days or weeks in your new school. Your induction will help you to familiarise yourself with your school and how it operates, and to be clear about what you need to do to fit into the workforce. It will help you to settle into your new job. Induction is also about both parties working together to make sure the employment relationship begins well. Induction is, in essence, a matching process. It brings school and teacher, teaching and new entrant together.

I only have my own experience to work with. How will I know if I am getting a good induction?
The answer to that is easier than you might think.

If you know who to turn to when you have a problem, if you know how to find the answers to your questions, if you are confident you can ask people in school for help without their judging you to be a nuisance, then you can be fairly certain you are getting a good induction. If you are confident that when you are faced with a crisis you will get support and guidance, then you will know the induction process in your school works well.

When I get to the end of my first year in teaching, should I consider my induction has finished?
When you get to the end of your first year, you should congratulate yourself. This is a landmark in your career. You know that the first year in teaching is the most difficult, and once you have got through it, you have made significant progress in your career as a teacher. If you have completed your probationary period satisfactorily, you can consider yourself to have moved on to the next stage in your career.

Whether or not you have completed your induction is another issue. Your induction aims to bring you up to competent worker standard. Thus, the job of induction is to enable you to do the job without needing extra support.

There will be aspects of your work where you still need to develop your expertise in order to reach that competent worker standard. Set yourself the task of doing so during your second year as a teacher.

Remember that in your first year you will have had extra support to help you to survive, a lighter timetable, an induction tutor or mentor and a degree of tolerance and understanding from your colleagues because you were new. As you move into your second year, more will be expected of you. You will be required to teach a full timetable, for example, and possibly to offer support to the next intake of newcomers. Are you ready for that change of status?

Perhaps the most sensible approach for you to take is to accept openly that you still have a lot to learn and you will still be grateful to receive help and support from your colleagues as you move into your second year. When you feel confident of your ability to deal with all aspects of your job, you can say that your induction had ended.

3.3   Survival strategies

Now you know that settling into a new job and a new role takes a lot of commitment on the part of every one concerned, you need to think about how you can do your bit to make your induction a success. Your most pressing questions almost certainly relate to your first term in teaching, or your first term in a new role. They can probably be summed up in one question:

How am I going to get through my first term?
The first thing you must do is to accept that your first term in teaching is going to be tough. You are new to your school. You are new to the profession. You are new to the specific role you have taken on. You are going to make mistakes. You are going to find that sometimes you don't know what to do. That's inevitable. You're going to find there is so much to do and so much to learn. It will often seem like you need to

learn everything immediately and do everything right at once.

You need a survival plan to help you to deal with this situation.

Your plan will be made up of a number of components. Your job will be to keep your plan in mind and never to lose track of it as you progress through your first term.

What will my survival plan look like?
Your plan will be made up of six elements, all of which are important but one is much more important than all the others. These elements are:

1. Avoid being overwhelmed by the job.
2. Get expert guidance when you need it.
3. Start to build your support network.
4. Learn from your mistakes.
5. Recognize what you are good at.
6. Keep your career options open.

You will need to work on all of these issues during your first year in teaching or in that new role. If you keep working on all six aspects of your plan, you will begin to create a positive impression of yourself, your abilities and your potential in your school. This will help you as you progress in teaching.

What is the most important element of my plan?
The answer to that is easy. If you are going to survive your first term, let alone get through your first year in teaching, you must ensure that you don't allow the job to overwhelm you. If you allow this to happen, you will very quickly lose sight of anything else you are trying to do.

However, this can be a difficult task. All teachers face the risk of being overwhelmed by the demands of the job. Teaching is a huge job. It can become an all-consuming job. It can take over your life, if you let it. It is very easy to be overwhelmed by your role as a teacher. It can creep up on you, and before you know where you are, you are drowning in a sea of tasks that must be done, deadlines that must be met, and classroom situations that you barely know how to handle.

You must focus on a strategy that prevents you from getting yourself into that situation, or if you find you have slipped into it, you must have a strategy that will help you to extricate yourself quickly, and with least damage to your confidence and standing in your school.

Getting through your first term will require you to remind yourself that however much is asked of you, you are a human being. However committed you are to becoming an effective teacher, you have a finite amount of resource to give to your new job. However great the temptation, don't allow yourself to work excessive hours on a regular basis. Working on school issues until late every night will exhaust you, as will working through weekends on marking and preparation. In the end you will achieve more, not less, if you set limits to the amount of time you allocate to your job.

Work hard. Work conscientiously, but remember you have a life outside your teaching life. You need to rest. You need to relax. You need to think about things other than teaching if you are to avoid becoming stale, over-worked and stressed.

Make sure you recognize the signs of the job beginning to overwhelm you. If you start to feel over-tired and listless, if you're feeling wound-up and stressed about your job, if you can't seem to switch off when you leave school in the evening, if you're bad-tempered and cross with every one, take action. Take a break. Do something different. If the problem persists, then seek professional advice, either from a trained and qualified counsellor or from your doctor.

Whatever you do, don't let this situation build up into a crisis. Keep a sense of proportion in your life. Remind yourself that you must keep on top of the job. If you don't, it will overwhelm you.

*I can make more time for myself and avoid being overwhelmed if I
cut out unnecessary meetings. Do I need to attend those sessions for
new teachers in school and at the teachers' centre?*
The answer is that you probably do need to attend, and you
would be unwise to judge these meetings to be unnecessary
or expendable.

It's always difficult to find time to fit everything into your
schedule. It's easy to convince yourself that you can miss a
workshop or a meeting, especially if it is held after school
and you need to travel somewhere to attend. Missing these
sessions can be a serious mistake.

Sessions for new teachers are often very useful in giving
you insights into the problems that every one who is new
to teaching faces, and guidance on how to deal with them.
You have the opportunity to meet different people at these
sessions, both new teachers like yourself and those who
support them. Taking part in meetings such as these can
help you to begin to build a network of people to whom you
can turn for support.

If, when you look at the agenda for the next scheduled
meeting, you think that what is going to be covered in a
session has little relevance to you, your situation and your
aspirations, it's probably still best to participate. At this stage
in your career, with your limited understanding of how
teaching works, and what you might need to learn about in
the future, you're probably not particularly well-placed to
make a decision about the value of what is being offered. So
play safe. Turn up and take part.

There is one type of meeting, however, that you would do
well to avoid. This is the session that offers nothing but an
opportunity to talk about how terrible a job teaching is, what
has gone wrong in people's classes, and how no one is doing
anything to help anybody. If a review of what isn't working is
not confined to the early part of a meeting, and if a session
does not move on to how to deal positively and con-
structively with the issues raised, then this is not the type of
session you want to take part in. This type of session won't
help you to move forward. In short, these meetings don't
add value to your work, so avoid them.

How do I find the expert guidance I need to help me survive?
Look around you. Use your eyes and ears. Be alert. To whom
do other teachers in school turn for advice? Where are the
acknowledged experts on behaviour issues, or on subject-
related issues, special educational needs or on assessment
practice? Find these people. Ask them questions. Go and
watch them teach. Learn from them.

If your school has assigned someone to help you through
your first term or your first year in teaching, make use of
that resource. Try to think ahead and ask for guidance
before you are faced with a perplexing issue. For example,
ask to go through your school's procedure for escorting
learners off-site before you have to do so yourself, not after
you have experienced difficulties on an expedition.

Find someone in school who is just a little more experienced than you and try to work closely with that person.
Watch carefully. You will learn a lot in an informal way just
by working alongside someone else.

Who else should I turn to for help?
The short answer is anyone you think can offer you assis-
tance. You should work hard at building up a support
network.

You are likely to get most help from the people working in
your school, so as well as the experts you are actively seeking
out, make sure you ask the school leader or manager who
has responsibility for your work for guidance. Also talk to
your fellow new starters or to the teachers who have been
teaching for one or two years. They will be able to help you
with very practical suggestions about what they are doing or
what they did to get through their early weeks and months
as teachers.

If you have a mentor, that is, someone who is assigned by
your school to help you to find your feet, build up a good
working relationship with him or her.

Outside school there may be new teachers in other local
schools with whom you can share experiences and hints and
tips.

Every one tells me I've got a lot to learn. How do I find the time to act on all the recommendations about what I should do to improve my practice?
You don't.

Accept that people will want to help you and will be making suggestions to you about what you should be doing. Thank anyone who offers you help and guidance. These colleagues are trying to help you and you should be grateful, but you should also recognize that you can't follow up every recommendation. If the advice is relevant, and if you think you can apply it, go ahead. Then give the people who have offered you the help some indication of how you have used their guidance.

However, throughout your teaching career you will find that people offer you guidance that in some cases does not fit your circumstances or the way in which you work. Begin now to differentiate between the type of support you find helpful and can use, and the type you can't.

Do I really need to read lots of books about teaching theory in my first year?
It will help you if you read something about good practice in teaching. You will, no doubt, have been recommended books in the past, and there will be some guides that you already value and some authors who you think are helpful.

You will already know something about your preferred learning style. You will know whether you like workbooks, case studies, theoretical texts, web-based learning, and so on. As you progress through your early weeks in teaching, or in a new role, you will also develop a sense of where you need to build up your expertise quickly. With so much available both in print and online, you will have plenty of information to work with.

Take a note of all the references people give you or which you find for yourself and set up a reading file. Read what you can, but accept that you can't follow up everything.

Since I'm new to teaching, how am I going to avoid making lots of terrible mistakes?
Accept now that you will make mistakes. Also remember that even the most experienced teacher makes mistakes, too. Put any mistakes into that context. No one is perfect. No one goes through life without making mistakes. You have unrealistic expectations if you think you can become a successful teacher without making mistakes.

The best thing to do is to think about mistakes in a positive way. Lots of people value mistakes and either treat them as pointers to learning, or redefine them as learning opportunities. People often say that the mistake itself is unimportant, provided that you learn from it. That's the main point. As a new teacher, as someone at the beginning of your life in teaching, provided you learn from your mistakes and don't repeat them, you will be making progress. Aim to do just that.

The smart move, however, will be to devise a plan which will help you to minimize your mistakes. Your success here depends on your gaining access to support and guidance from a range of people in school from your first days in your job. It also requires you to be very clear about what you will do differently to help you to avoid making the same mistake more than once.

This is where you can really help yourself. Take time to analyse *why* something has gone wrong and *what* you intend to do differently next time you are faced with a similar situation. As you make your plans take advice from experts in your school. Then work out exactly *how* you will approach an issue next time you have to deal with it.

Teaching isn't for me. I know it isn't. What can I do?
Don't jump to that conclusion. You might not like being a teacher right now, but that doesn't mean you have made a bad career choice in becoming a teacher.

If you have only been a teacher for a short period, you need to think about how you can be sure you don't want to be a teacher. You may have ended up in the wrong job. You may not be getting the sort of support you really need as a new entrant. Your induction programme might be inadequate. You might also have chosen a school where the organizational culture does not fit your preferred way of working. You might not get on with your head of department or some of the senior people. All of these are unfortunate circumstances, but they relate to the school in which you are working. They should not lead you to make a decision that teaching is not right for you. If you worked in another school, you might think quite differently.

Think also about your own expectations of yourself. Are you being over-ambitious about what you can achieve in your early months as a teacher? It takes time to become a competent teacher, and longer still to become a good teacher. Are you expecting too much of yourself, too soon? If, in your first term, you manage to keep your head above water, you are making good progress.

Being a teacher is difficult to begin with, but it does get easier – and quite quickly, too. Set yourself a deadline by when you expect things to improve. Use the advice in this chapter to help you to make things better. Don't make a hasty decision about the quality of your career choice.

3.4 Finding your very special talents

Even though you are still at the beginning of your life as a teacher, or new to your role, you should try to recognize what you do well and what you enjoy doing, as well as thinking about the areas where you need to improve your practice quickly. You must remember that although you are new, you have a valuable contribution to make, now and in the future. You have skills and you have expertise, so be aware of your talents.

It seems a silly question, but how will I know what I do well?
First, you will know when you are pleased with how something has gone. Your own judgement is a very valuable indicator of your success here.

You should also look for feedback on what you are doing. There are three main ways in which people tell you they think you are doing well and that they value what you do. These are:

- offering endorsement of what you have done
- seeking your help, guidance and support
- offering you the opportunity to lead on something you do well.

Note first people's **endorsement** of what you do – this is an indicator of approval.

For example, if someone congratulates you on having made an excellent presentation, this is an endorsement of what you do. If your head of department, or someone similar, has made the statement after watching you teach a lesson, you need to find out what, specifically, he or she liked. Ask for more information. What is being endorsed? Is it the mix of approaches you used? Is it the way you used formal presentation, questions and answers, visual reinforcement of your message, etc? Find out.

Then think about how and when people ask you for **help, guidance and support** when they are doing things that they have acknowledged you do well – this is an indicator of their confidence in your abilities.

For example, if your classroom is really well organized and a colleague asks how to make his or her classroom look as good as yours, this is a request for support. Once again, ask for specifics. Is it the overall impression your classroom creates that your colleague likes? Is it the way displays are organized? What does your colleague want help with?

Finally, note the occasions on which you are asked to take a **lead** in an area where it is known in school that you have expertise – this indicates that you are an acknowledged expert in something.

For example, you are asked by the person in charge if you can help your work team – your department, your year, your key stage – to organize its assignments more effectively. Find out what the people in the team value about the way you work. Are your assignments all well ordered? Are they easily accessed and well referenced? Are you achieving more, with your assignments, than are some of your colleagues?

In addition, always note when people congratulate you on what you are doing. Don't brush people's statements on your successes aside. Don't undervalue people's judgements of you.

You can also use the support mechanisms in your school, such as your progress reviews, to help you to be clear on your successes and to get feedback on what you are doing well.

How exactly can I use my progress reviews to help me to be aware of what I do well?

In your first year in teaching, or in your first year in any new role, you are likely to have progress reviews with someone senior to yourself in your school. There is always a tendency for such reviews to be taken up with day-to-day operational issues, problems that have arisen, crises in school, etc., and to focus on next steps, damage limitation and getting through to the end of term.

Ensure that some part of these meetings is also allocated to reviewing your successes and to discussing how you can build on your successes. If you have found an activity, by design or by chance, that you do well, discuss it. Discuss ways of ensuring you have more opportunities to do the things you do well. Build on your success. If you can, try to get some feedback on how your successes compare with those of the mythical 'typical' new entrant to teaching or the new post holder.

There are lots of options open to me. Is it too early for me to start to specialize?

Probably.

This doesn't mean you should let opportunities to get involved in projects pass you by. It does mean you should avoid focusing on one or two areas where you think you would like to develop your expertise, to the exclusion of others.

Use your reviews with senior people in school, and draw

on the expertise of other teachers you know, to find out more about as many different specialisms within teaching as you can identify. You will find there are lots to choose from. Make sure you are aware of a good range of possible career paths before you make any decisions about specialization.

Do your best, at this stage in your career, to keep as many different options for your future development open as possible. Some people describe progress through a career as being akin to walking along a corridor where doors are opening and closing all the time. You just need to make certain you are not closing doors that ought to remain open, or that you avoid looking into rooms where the doors are open and where you might find something of interest.

How will I know what to ask to do more of next year?
Think about what interests you and what you do well. If you find that you also like the tasks that you do well, then you are on your way towards shaping your second year in teaching, or in your new role, and possibly your future career.

Talk about your next steps in teaching to people in your school, to the person responsible for your reviews, to your line manager, to your colleagues and so on. Gather a range of opinions about how you might shape the next stage in your career as well as thinking about your own preferences.

If you're still not sure about where to begin to focus your efforts, then you can afford to wait a little longer before you make any decisions. Far better to delay a development decision for a little while than to start along a career path that is not right for you.

Summary

1. This chapter is for teachers at the beginning of their careers and for teachers taking on new roles.
2. This chapter will help teachers to use their initial experiences in teaching to begin to shape their careers.

3. Induction is important for all those who are new to teaching and new to their roles.
4. Induction aims to bring new entrants and people taking on new responsibilities up to competent worker standard quickly.
5. A good induction will ensure that new teachers, and those taking on new responsibilities, get the support and guidance they need to help them to fulfil their responsibilities.
6. New teachers should produce a survival plan to help them to get through their early weeks and months in teaching.
7. If they are going to survive in teaching, new teachers must find ways to avoid being overwhelmed by the job.
8. Teachers need to seek out expert guidance to help them to avoid making serious mistakes.
9. New teachers should also work out what they are good at. They can do this by noting where people in school endorse what they are doing, seek their advice and guidance or ask them to lead on a task or project.
10. Teachers should avoid specialization too early in their careers in order to keep as many career options available to them as possible.

Activities

Two activities follow which are linked to the key messages of this chapter. The first will help you to produce your survival plan. The second will help you to decide what you are good at, and what people in your school value about your contribution.

Activity one – Creating your survival plan

Overview

This chapter strongly recommends teachers produce a survival plan to help them to get through their first weeks and

months in teaching or in their new role. This activity will
help you to produce such a plan.

Task

Make a copy of the table opposite. You will see that the six
survival strategies have been set out in the leftmost column.
Questions from the chapter have been linked to each of the
survival strategies and set out in the middle column.

1. Look at each survival strategy in turn. Re-read the
    responses to the questions in the chapter which are
    linked to the survival strategy. Think about how you
    can use the advice. Then note an action you intend to
    take, linked to each of the survival strategies, in the
    final column of the table you have drawn.
2. Now select the two activities from your list of proposed
    actions which you think you should complete imme-
    diately. Highlight these actions.
3. What benefits do you think you will gain as a result of
    completing these actions?
4. How are you going to make sure you now complete
    these two actions? Record your decisions and keep
    your notes safe. Refer to them each week until you
    have completed the actions.

Survival strategies

Survival strategy	Questions linked to this strategy	Your proposed action
1. Avoid being overwhelmed by the job	I can make more time for myself and avoid being overwhelmed if I cut out unnecessary meetings. Do I need to attend those sessions for new teachers in school and at the teachers' centre? Every one tells me I've a lot to learn. How do I find the time to act on all the recommendations about what I should do to improve my practice?	
2. Get expert guidance when you need it	How do I find the expert guidance I need to help me survive?	
3. Start to build your support network	Who else should I turn to for help?	
4. Learn from your mistakes	Since I'm new to teaching, how am I going to avoid making lots of terrible mistakes?	
5. Recognize what you are good at	It seems a silly question. But how will I know what I do well? How exactly can I use my progress reviews to help me to be aware of what I do well? How will I know what to ask to do more of next year?	
6. Keep your career options open	There are lots of options open to me. Is it too early for me to start to specialize?	

Activity two – Finding your very special talents

Overview

If you are going to manage your career successfully, you need an accurate understanding of what you are good at. Sometimes it's easy to work out. Sometimes it isn't.

Therefore, make a point of gathering information about what every one you work with values about your contribution to school life. This will help you to know what to draw attention to when you are applying for promotion. It will help you to steer performance review and appraisal discussions in the right direction. It will also help you to be clear about the achievements you have every right to be proud of.

Task

1. To help you to find your very special talents, set up a system of recording how staff in your school:
   - endorse what you do
   - ask you for help, guidance and support
   - ask you to lead on specific projects or tasks.
2. Make sure you capture the observations about your work that people make. Keep a log, possibly like the one shown opposite, and update it regularly. Make sure you note:
   a. what is being said about you
   b. who is making the statement
   c. the context in which the statement is being made
   d. what exactly is being approved? *(You may need to ask the person making the observation to give you more detail in order to be certain.)*
3. Each month, or each term, look for trends in what people value about your contribution. This will help you to identify your very special talents.
4. Make notes about what you find.

Refer to the notes you have made when completing these activities whenever you are thinking about your career aspirations and your career goals.

My very special talents

What exactly was said? (Typical statements include …)	Date on which the statement was made	Made by (status of person)	Context in which the statement was made	Which aspect of my practice was being approved?
Endorsement				
You did that well …				
What you did was a great success …				
I like the way you …				
Thank you for doing …				
Guidance				
How do I do what you have done?				
What's your opinion on how I should …				
Tell me how you achieved that.				
Show me how …				
Explain to me how …				
Take me through …				
Leadership				
Can you help us all to do this?				
Can you set down the process for us?				
Can you give a presentation to … about …				
Can you help us when we go wrong?				

Chapter Four

Developing your career

4.1 Overview

This chapter is for teachers looking to begin to shape their teaching careers.

It will help you to establish how you want to develop your career and to produce an action plan that will help you to reach your career goals. It will help you to develop an understanding of what career success will mean for you, whether you are thinking about promotion or not.

Use this chapter at any point in your teaching career. Use it when you are approaching the end of your first year in teaching. Use it when you first think about looking for a different role, but have not decided what sort of change you are looking for. Use it to help you to assess, or to reassess, what you want out of your teaching career. Use it to help you to be clear about the type of career within teaching that will help you to feel satisfied with your working life. Use it to help you to find the career path that is right for you, to produce an action plan to help you to travel along that path – and to keep to it.

Use this chapter also when you are preparing for your performance review or appraisal.

If you have defined your career aspirations, and if you have already established some career goals as a result of working through Chapter Two, this chapter will help you to create, and implement, a career action plan to help you to achieve those goals.

If you don't have any goals, and if you don't want to think about goals at the moment, this chapter will help you to make sense of the present state of your career and to manage your progress to the next point in your development journey.

The chapter is divided into three further parts:

- establishing your development route
- developing your career
- finding the right school.

You will find questions that teachers thinking about how best to develop their careers often ask themselves under each of these headings. Review the answers as you work through the chapter and judge how relevant they are to your circumstances.

4.2   Establishing your development route

Developing your career. Progressing your career. Taking your career forward. Moving ahead. These are the sort of statements teachers make when they are thinking about how they intend to manage their careers. All the statements are about change and movement, and once you have made a start to your teaching career, or arrived at a point where you think it is time to review your progress to date, you will need to decide where you want travel in teaching and how you intend to get there.

It's important to make sure you avoid travelling in the wrong direction, making detours and needing to backtrack. Plan carefully to ensure you move your career in the direction that is right for you.

There's such a lot I could do, where do I start?
Practical activities are always a good way to start on a new project. Putting yourself in charge of your career is no exception.

Start by thinking about what you like doing and what you're good at. Look for opportunities to spend more of your working time doing these things. Remember it's often possible to shape your existing role to fit your preferences and interests. This is one of the advantages people working in professional roles have. Moulding your current job to suit your preferences is often as simple as volunteering to take on particular tasks or stating clearly where your interests lie.

Wherever possible make an effort to shape your current role to suit your development plans, because by doing this you will be broadening your experience in ways that will be useful to you later, but without the upheaval of a change of job. Look for opportunities to spend even more of your time doing what you like and what you're good at when you think about applying for jobs and promotions.

You should also look ahead and decide what you believe you might find interesting in teaching. Think about what you would like to know more about, what else you would like to be able to do or which skills you would like to gain. Do this to help you to work more effectively in your current role and to prepare for a role you would like to take on in the future.

Try to formulate career goals if you haven't done so already. Set down goals which help you to be clear about where you want to be in your career in three to five years' time.

If you find your career goals and your interests and what you're good at all fit together, you can now proceed to work on your career action plan. If not, you still have some work to do on goal setting. Use Chapter Two to help you with this task.

Do I need to think about specialization now?
Sooner or later you will probably decide to specialize. Whether or not you are looking for promotion you will develop interests which you will want to pursue. You will find areas of expertise that you will want to know more about. If you want to remain a classroom teacher, you will probably want to extend your skills in particular aspects of classroom management practice as you become more experienced. You will need to keep up to date with developments in teaching and learning practice. You will also be looking to be able to extend your capabilities, if you decide to seek promotion.

You would be wise to try to avoid closing off development avenues as you think about specialization. Just because you have an interest in assessment, or you want to know more about the learning styles of the fourteen to nineteen age group, or the challenges linked to teaching numeracy, does not mean you should abandon your interest in other aspects of teaching. Maintain your knowledge and understanding of more than one area in order to avoid being labelled as someone who is only interested in one thing, and, by implication, someone who will only be considered for development opportunities in that one area.

How can I make sure I am considering a broad enough range of development routes?
You are already thinking about the areas where you have expertise and the areas in which you like working.

You also need to be aware of how schools are organized. Most schools have academic and pastoral specialisms. There are also whole school functions, for example, assessment or special needs, as well as whole school leadership roles. Choosing to work in some areas will take you out of the classroom. Choosing other areas will ensure you remain teaching and learning based.

Do an analysis of the types of specialisms in your own school and those which are advertised in the educational press or on websites. This will help you to gain an understanding of the breadth of development opportunities available to teachers.

Once you identify a new area that interests you, find someone who has expertise in that area. Ask about the work. Find out what it is like to work in jobs linked to that type of expertise. Then make your decision about whether this is the right area in which you wish to develop your career.

Remember that you can look beyond a career built on taking up full-time, permanent posts if you choose to develop your career in that way. You may wish to consider a fixed-term contract that offers the type of experience you are seeking, or look at opportunities for working abroad.

Does thinking about the right development route mean that I will also need to think about continuous professional development (CPD)?

Yes, it does.

You will need to think about continuous professional development (CPD) throughout your teaching career and make sure you have access to what you need. Whatever skills and expertise you have now, you will need to develop your expertise in the future. Jobs change around you. New initiatives arrive. You need to make sure you do not become stale in your approaches to teaching and learning, and you need to make sure you remain aware of developments in your field.

CPD is not an option. It is an essential aspect of being a teacher.

How much CPD do I need?

You should bear in mind two principles when you think about what is absolutely necessary in terms of your CPD.

First, whenever you take on a new responsibility, you will need an induction. Every one, from head teachers, to heads of year, to subject co-ordinators, to examinations specialists, all need an induction when they take on a new role. Induction is the means by which you arrive at competent worker standard. You can't just walk into a new role and do it well. Always look for an induction when you take on any new responsibility, and ask for one if it isn't automatically offered to you.

You also need to think about CPD to enable you to keep on top of your job. Whether or not you are looking for promotion, you will need to remain aware of new syllabuses, new assessment methods, changing subject matter, different ways of teaching and so on. Sometimes you will do your updating on your own, through reading the relevant journals and talking to your colleagues. Sometimes you will attend formal training. Sometimes your school will arrange in-house training for you and for others. The mix of approaches is not too important, but maintaining your ability to do your job is. This is the means by which you sustain your employability, an essential element of your work as a teacher.

Beyond this essential CPD you will also be thinking about CPD to help you to fulfil your career aspirations and your career goals. How much of this type of CPD you undertake is your choice. It could encompass higher-level qualifications, secondments, in education or in industry, work-based learning projects and many more ways of learning.

Will I need a higher degree?

It's an interesting question. The answer depends as much on your personal preferences as on the career destination, or career goal, you have in mind.

People decide to study for higher degrees for three principal reasons. These are:

- to advance their understanding of a subject area or discipline that they are enthusiastic to learn more about
- intellectual challenge
- to advance their careers.

Following a higher degree programme is a major under-taking. It could take years to complete, especially if you try to combine it with teaching full time. You must make sure you know why you are planning to follow a major study programme and what you hope to gain from it before you even think about enrolling.

Your reason for committing to a programme of study will usually dictate the degree chosen and the benefits that you are likely to gain from your studies. If you are looking to develop an in-depth knowledge of an aspect of your work, whether this is linked to teaching and learning or to your subject specialism, then the benefits you gain may help you with your career, but there is a good chance that those benefits will be primarily personal.

If you are looking to become a head teacher, you will almost certainly be thinking about a higher degree linked to aspects of leadership to help you to advance your career. If you are thinking about studying to stretch your intellectual capabilities, then you may decide to study something unrelated to your work.

However, you are more likely to become disillusioned, and fail to complete your programme, if you choose a programme without really knowing why you want to study, so think carefully before you act.

4.3 Developing your career

Having thought about your development in broad terms, you should now think seriously about career planning and how you are going to progress your career, irrespective of whether or not you are actively seeking promotion.

Now is the time to focus again on your career aspirations and career goals and to devise your career action plan and the implementation strategy that will help you to fulfil your plan.

Do I really need career goals?
If you are going to put yourself in charge of your career, yes, you do. Have a look at Chapter Two if you have not already thought about your career aspirations, your career goals and what motivates you.

What do I do once I have my career goals?
The next step is to turn those career goals into an action plan which will be supported by an implementation strategy. Having an action plan will help you to be clear about *what* steps you need to take to reach your career goals. Your implementation strategy will set out *how* you intend to ensure those actions are completed.

I can see I need an action plan, but how will having an implementation strategy help me?
Teachers are good at planning. They plan is many different areas of their working lives. They produce teaching plans,

post-inspection action plans, curriculum plans, professional development plans, school improvement plans and so on. These plans are full of who, what and when statements. They also include statements about resources needed to fulfil the plans and so on. Yet, as most teachers know, there are action plans gathering dust in cupboards and filing cabinets in most schools, lying forgotten along with a host of New Year's Resolutions and lists of objectives and targets.

You know that plans have their uses. They are excellent starting points. Your plan will help you to be clear about what you intend to do, but every plan also needs an implementation strategy. Your implementation strategy shows how you intend to address the activities in your plan, how you intend to turn your plan into reality.

What will go into my action plan?
Quite simply your action plan sets out what you intend to do to reach your goals. It is a list of activities, wherever possible set out in date order or the order in which you need to complete them. Your plan may comprise a list of things you need to do to be ready to apply for a post that will take you nearer to reaching one of your goals, or gaining that post might be the goal itself. There may be one step in your action plan. There may be several.

Your action plan will set out a timetable for your actions and set deadlines for its completion. It will also deal with how you intend to resource your actions.

And what goes into my implementation strategy?
Your implementation strategy sets out how you intend to ensure you complete the activities you nominate in your action plan. It is a practical statement. For example, if you have set yourself the task of taking on a particular role as the next move in your career, and noted this in your action plan, then in your implementation strategy you will consider how you are going to get any experience you need to be ready to apply for that role, or how you are going to manage to find time to study for any qualifications you have decided you need to be ready to be considered for the role you want.

Why is it important to include a timetable for action?
You need a timetable for all your activities so that you can keep track of how you are progressing. Without a timetable, and without deadlines, you could drift for years, always finding a reason for avoiding action. A timetable for action will focus you on what you are going to do to fulfil your career goals and to complete the activities you have put in your action plan.

To create your timetable, estimate how long it is going to take you to reach your career goals. Make a detailed time-table for action for the current term, for the current year and further ahead if you can. Be very clear on what you intend to achieve by when, but remember, the further away from the present you are planning, the greater the margin of error.

Take care when you think about the time needed to implement your plans. Planning presents problems for many teachers because they set unrealistic deadlines for action in the plans they produce. As a result, they often fail to complete their plans.

What sort of resources do I need to fulfil my action plan?
Remember that everything costs. Part of your planning process will be about allocating resource to your plan. If you don't resource your plan appropriately, you are unlikely to complete the actions and get to the destination you say you want to reach.

Resource in the context of career planning must include the personal resource you are prepared to give to fulfil your plan. It also includes the external resource you will need to draw on to succeed. You must also consider how you intend to secure all the resource you need to fulfil your plan.
Personal resource – is about the time and effort you are prepared to put into the task of reaching your goals. Progressing your career will sometimes involve change to your working life and to your life outside work. It could mean learning new skills. It could mean gaining additional qualifications. It could mean taking time out of your current role in order to gain specific experience in a new field. The

changes you need to make could involve personal sacrifice, for example, loss of leisure time, and a significant investment in terms of time and possibly in terms of money.

Sometimes you may wish to progress your career in a way that means your school or your employing authority is unable to support you. This might require you to finance some of your development yourself.

External resource – is primarily about drawing on the guidance and insights of others to help you to complete the actions you have put in your plan.

It's often difficult to be realistic about your own plans and to see the flaws and shortcomings in what you are proposing. Therefore, you should not work in isolation. Include others in your career planning activities. Seek out feedback and guidance from people working in a variety of roles. Other people can provide you with valuable insights that will help you to refine your thoughts before you become too committed to a course of action. Using external resource in this way will help you to produce realistic action plans and implementation strategies

Who are the best people to help me to plan my career?
Your networks are your best source of support. You will have built, or be building, a number of support networks. Draw on the expertise of all of them. The most important of these are:

your personal support network – your family and friends, the people who are important to you in your life, the people who matter to you. It's a big mistake to plan your career without taking these people's views into account. They know you and are well placed to help you with your planning process. You also need to consider these people's wishes because their needs and expectations will affect your ability to fulfil any plan you make.

your professional support network – the people who know you and your work who you would trust with information about your aspirations and plans. These include your colleagues and ex-colleagues with whom you have maintained contact. People from outside teaching can also offer you guidance and should be included in your network. Every teacher needs a professional support network, so if you have not begun to build one, start now.

your network of professional advisers – experts from within teaching and beyond to whom you turn for guidance about their area of expertise. These will include people already working in the roles you aspire to hold, financial advisers, including pensions advisers, and those who advise you on legal and medical matters.

Calling on the support of people from all of these groups can help you to make your career action plan and implementation strategy more robust.

It's a good idea to take advice from more than one source so that you will have the benefit of a variety of opinions. As with all advice, it's your choice whether or not you take it, especially when the people you consult offer conflicting opinions. However, where you find several people offer you similar guidance, you will need to think seriously before turning it down.

How do I decide who should form part of my professional support network?
Include people whose advice you will value and from whom you will be happy to accept feedback. Make sure the people you choose are willing to offer you feedback, too. If you find people are reluctant to help you, respect their choice and look elsewhere for guidance.

How many people should I aim to bring into my support networks?
There is no single right answer here.

However, you need a range of people with different talents, experience and expertise. You will approach different people about different career management issues. You are unlikely to call on every one in your networks when you reach a major decision point in your career and you are thinking about what to do next.

Some people will be part of one of your networks because you call on them for expert advice. Some will be in a network because they have known you a long time, or because you know them well. Some people will be in your networks because you are close to them. In the end the choice of how many people you draw into your career management process is yours.

What do I do if I get lots of different advice?
Cheer! That's exactly what you want. You have developed networks to enable you to get advice from people with varied experience and varied perspectives. If their views are diverse, and if members of your networks think of issues and options which you haven't, then that is to your benefit.

Listen to the advice. Value it. Then use it to help you to arrive at your own decisions.

That sounds complicated. Do I need to do all this?
If you are going to stand the best chance of arriving at the right career destination, and of being in charge of your career, then, yes, you do.

What do people get wrong when they plan their careers?
The most common mistake that people – including teachers – make is to think about their careers in isolation from the rest of their lives. They set their career goals and plan their careers without taking into consideration what is happening in their lives outside teaching.

What is going on in your relationships and what is happening to people who are important to you will affect your career and the amount of time you have to devote to your responsibilities, your own professional development and to making your way in your career. If you don't take these issues into account, you could find events in your life outside work suddenly forcing you to change direction and throwing any plans you have made into disarray.

What else could stop me completing all the actions I plan?
Events. The unexpected. Changes in your circumstances. Any number of things.

If you are wise you will produce a contingency plan to take account of such occurrences. This will help you to deal with what could get in the way of your completing your plan. Think about what you would do if something unexpected happened. Then consider the 'what ifs' you think are most likely to occur, and the ones that could most readily prevent you from fulfilling your plan.

When considering these challenges, think first about changes that could happen to you as an individual. These changes may relate to your health, your level of personal commitment to fulfilling your plan, your belief in your ability to fulfil your plan or your willingness to allow yourself to succeed. You will also find you want different things at different stages in your life and your work might become more, or less, important to you as you move through life.

Also think about your circumstances. You may need to shape your career planning activities with reference to the needs and expectations of others. What you believe is required of you in your career could be affected by the levels of personal and household debt you carry, your commitments to house purchases or by the financial demands placed on you by your family.

Your responsibilities to others, including caring responsibilities for your spouse, for elderly relatives and for your children could also affect how you plan and manage your career. You may find that you experience sudden changes in your circumstances, for example, dealing with the death of a close relative, the break-up of a relationship or moving house.

Think about the implications of the 'what ifs' that are most likely to occur whenever you review your career plan. Think about how you might react when faced with these specific challenges. That way you stand a better chance of reaching your career destinations.

If I think I'm now ready to produce an action plan and an implementation strategy, what do I do?
Look at Chapter Eight.

That chapter sets out guidance on how to direct your whole career management process.

How will I know when I am succeeding?
This is the easy part.

By formulating your career goals you have already set out your definition of success. You can measure your success in terms of reaching your goals and with reference to how much closer you are to achieving your goals after you complete each activity in your career action plan.

You can also judge your success by reviewing how you feel about your teaching career. Are you enjoying your work? Is your work bringing you personal satisfaction? If it is, that's great. If it isn't, then it's probably time to look again at your career goals, or at how you manage the relationship between your working life and your life outside work and revise your action plan as necessary.

You could also think about what motivates you. Chapter Two dealt with four important motivators: reward, recognition, personal development and learning, and helping others. Is what you are doing in tune with your motivation? If it is, you will find you value your successes more highly. If your answers suggest that you might want to consider a change in direction, as far as your career is concerned, then read Chapter Six once you have finished working through this chapter.

These strategies, used either singly or in combination, should give you a satisfactory means of reviewing your career management process.

4.4   Finding the right school

It's important that you don't just focus on yourself when you are planning your career. The school in which you work is also important. Schools vary enormously so you must take care when choosing one. You will progress your career most effectively if you work in the sort of school that suits your values, your temperament as well as your preferred working style.

I thought I just looked for the job that is right for me. Why do I need to choose the schools carefully, too?
You should always think about the school as well as the job when you are considering taking on a new role. The teaching role you accept, and the environment in which you work, are components of the same career management equation. If you are going to progress your career effectively – and that can mean in terms of promotion, achievement in a particular role, job satisfaction or any other success criterion you nominate – you need to be doing the right job in the right working environment. You will know fairly soon in your career which sort of working environment you are looking for. It will be one in which you can most readily use your preferred way of working.

Every organization has its own culture, often described as the way things are done there. For example, some schools are very formal, with policies for everything and handbooks and procedures to ensure you complete every task in the defined manner. You will encounter problems in this sort of school if you try to do things differently from the established way of working. If you persist in doing things in your own way, you will get a reputation for being difficult. You might be categorized as someone who is not a team player or who does not fit in.

Some schools, while having a framework for key tasks, leave plenty of scope for you to define your own way of working. It's much easier for you to change things and to innovate in this type of school. You are more likely to be able to try out new ideas without needing to seek permission from several people, if you work here.

Then there are schools which combine the formal and the rigid with the informal, where different senior managers have different ways of organizing work and for managing change and innovation.

There are some schools that change their culture almost overnight, when a new head teacher arrives, for example.

You should take the working environment into account whenever you are thinking about taking up a post in a particular school, simply because you won't be happy and you won't achieve as much if you find yourself working in an environment to which you are not well suited.

How will I find the right sort of school for me?
There is no hard and fast way of judging schools but one of the most important things you need to know to help you to make your decision is how formal or informal a school is. Talking to the head teacher and senior staff about how they planned for their most recent inspection, or asking how they manage their relationship with their governing body and the local community, will give you an idea of the leadership style. These issues, in turn, will affect how the school is managed and how you are likely to be treated, if you decide to work there.

Finding out about how teaching is organized and how the curriculum is planned will also help you to gain an understanding of the organizational culture. And, of course, talking to the staff who work there about how they order stock, how they plan events or how they manage their own development can give you some further useful insights.

I know I want to move to a different part of the country. How can I investigate a school when I work a long way away from it?
You need to find a way.

In your case you are considering doing far more than simply changing your school. You are thinking about an upheaval that could involve a house purchase, uprooting your family and making a major change in your life. It is important that you check out the working environment, as well as the job, because once you have made your move you could be living at that new location for a long time.

If you make a mistake, taking a step back or changing course again could be difficult for you, especially if you have your own children's education and the needs of close relatives to take into account when you consider moving again.

Do some internet searches. Find out as much as you can about the school. Ring them up and talk to the right people. If you request a job description, then there is a good chance you will also be sent an organization chart, so you will know which role holders it would be advisable to speak to. If at all possible, visit the school. Be prepared to finance the trip yourself. Doing so might save you a lot of money in the long run.

I'm worried about ending up in the sort of school where the workload will be enormous. How do I avoid this?
Teacher workload is a problem that doesn't ever seem to go away, so wherever you go you will find there is plenty to do. There will be more calls on your time than you have hours in the day. That's something that every one faces who works in what are known as caring professions. You will have to find ways of dealing with workload management if you are going to have a successful and rewarding teaching career and if you are going to put yourself in charge of your career.

If you are really worried about workload issues, try to find schools which take work–life balance seriously. This means looking for schools which have a work–life balance policy and which take steps to help their staff to avoid work-related stress.

Look for schools where work–life balance and teacher workload are regularly on the management agenda and where senior people are actively working to help staff to avoid overload and excessive working hours.

When you investigate, do you find that people are in school early in the morning and late into the evening on a regular basis? Does every one stay in school until the head goes home? If they do, these are warning signs you should not ignore. Ask yourself this question: will you be able to opt out of the long hours culture if you take a job there?

How much should I take a school's reputation into account when trying to decide where I want to work?
A school's reputation is important. It's helpful to work in a school which is successful and has a good reputation. When you say you work in such a school, you will be judged by others to be one of the people who is contributing to its success, so some of the positive regard that people give to the school will rub off on you.

You should always try to find out about the reputation of any school you are thinking of working in. You need to know how it has done in its recent inspections. You need to know something about its staff turnover, including how long the current head teacher has been in post. You need to find out if it is over-subscribed. Check if the school is regularly in the news, either locally or nationally, and why. Find out what local people, both those working in education and those working in other sections of the economy, think about it.

Armed with that information, much of which can be gained via the internet, you can begin to think about how working in a particular school will help you to take your career in the direction in which you wish to proceed. You will need to think about your career goals and your career action plan when making these decisions.

Sometimes, you will choose to take on a role in a school that is experiencing difficulties, if you think you have a contribution to make there. If you think working in a less successful school will advance your career, or give you opportunities to try out new approaches to dealing with particular problems, or help you to progress your career in some other way, then you may decide to take a job there.

Just as with every career decision, you will need to know why you are making a particular choice now and how it will help you to achieve your career goals in the future.

Summary

1. This chapter is for teachers looking to develop and shape their careers.
2. It can be used by teachers at any point in their teaching careers.
3. The chapter looks at how to plan a development route in teaching and how to choose the right school in which to work.
4. Teachers looking to develop their careers, whether or not they are interested in promotion, should ensure

they are aware of the full range of development options open to them.

5. When progressing their careers, wherever possible, teachers should begin by trying to shape their present role to fit their preferences and interests.
6. Sooner or later teachers will need to consider specialization.
7. Continuous professional development (CPD) is essential in every teacher's career.
8. Teachers need an action plan to help them to fulfil their career aspirations and to reach their career goals. They also need an implementation strategy, a contingency plan and a means of reviewing their success in fulfilling their action plans.
9. Teachers need support networks to help them to produce realistic and achievable action plans.
10. The most common mistake teachers make when planning their careers is to forget that their lives outside their work will affect their careers.
11. Finding the right school is also important and teachers should seek out schools where the organizational culture matches their preferred working styles.
12. Teachers should take into account such issues as a school's reputation and how it helps teachers to manage their workload when choosing a school in which to work.

Activities

Two activities follow which are linked to the major themes of this chapter. The first will help you to develop and build effective support networks. The second will help you to produce a realistic and achievable career action plan and implementation strategy.

Activity one – Building your support networks

Overview

Your professional support network and your personal support network will both be valuable to you as you work to manage your career effectively.

In this activity you are asked to identify a number of individuals from within your networks who you would consult if you were thinking about a range of career decisions. If you find you do not have people in your network who you might consult about any of these specific issues, consider how to extend your network to include at least one person who could help you if you were in this situation.

In each instance you may decide that you would approach more than one person.

Task

1. With which people in your professional support and personal support networks would you discuss your ideas if you were:
   a. actively seeking promotion
   b. looking to change the direction of your career
   c. changing schools
   d. moving to a different part of the country
   e. struggling to meet your performance targets
   f. having problems with discipline in school
   g. in dispute with a senior staff member in school
   h. experiencing difficulties in a relationship outside school
   i. in debt and struggling to manage your repayments
   j. worried about your health
   k. worried about the health of someone close to you
   l. disillusioned with teaching.
   Make a note of your choices and keep your notes safe.
2. Now think briefly about how large your two networks will need to be to ensure you can call on support in all of the above cases.
   Is it: 1, 2, 4, 8, 16, 32, 64 or more people?

3. As a result of completing this activity, do you think you
   need to extend the scope of any of your support networks? If you do, draw up a list of all the people who
   you would like to include in your support networks.
   Think also about how you are going to encourage
   them to support your career management strategy.

Activity two – Defining an action plan

Overview

One of the major problems teachers experience with career
planning is that they produce career action plans which are
unrealistic. They often omit essential steps along the way
and produce timetables for achieving their objectives which
are too optimistic. This activity will help with your career
management timetable and with assessing your readiness to
take on the roles you wish to hold.

Task

Planning your career from only your own perspective is a
high-risk strategy. Seeking out feedback on your career
goals, and the career journey you intend to make to reach
your goals, is an essential part of the career planning
process.

1. Review the following questions and think, first, about
   how you would answer them if you had a specific role
   in mind and you were advising yourself about your
   career. Note down your responses and keep them
   safe.
   • If someone at my level in teaching wanted to
     become *(specify role)*, how long do you think it
     would take?
   • If someone at my level in teaching wanted to
     become *(specify role)*, how many career moves do
     you think it would take to get there?

- What experience do you think someone in *(specify role)* needs to be ready to do this job?
- What qualifications do you think someone in *(specify role)* needs to be ready to do this job?
- What advice would you give someone like me looking to become a *(specify role)*?

2. Now think about your professional support network and your personal support network. Answer the following questions and make a note of your answers. Keep your responses safe.
   - Which of your colleagues do you intend to ask these questions?
   - Which of the managers and leaders in your school will you ask these questions?
   - Which people who already hold the responsibility you wish to take on will you ask these questions?
   - Which people who know you well will you ask these questions?
   - Which people who are not part of the teaching profession will you ask these questions?
   - Who else should you ask?
3. Ask the questions of the people you have nominated. Note their responses and keep their replies safe.
4. Decide how you will use the information you have gathered to support your career planning process.
5. Now produce an action plan to help you to define the route to the role you have been considering. *(Say how you will resource your development activities and how long it will take you to gain that role. Consider any additional experience or further training you might need.)*
6. Set out your implementation strategy. *(Explain how you are going to complete the actions you are nominated. Where will you find the time? How will you gain any additional experience you need? Which training will you undertake and when?)*
7. Produce a contingency plan. Think about what could get in the way of your completing your action plan and consider how you are going to avoid, or overcome, setbacks.

Refer to the notes you have made when completing both activities whenever you are thinking about your career action plan and your implementation strategy.

Chapter Five

Seeking promotion

5.1 Overview

This chapter is for teachers who have decided that they are looking for promotion.

It will help you to be clear about what to do to gain promotion within education. It will help you to understand how best to advance your career and to remain satisfied with your career management strategy. It will also help you to get back on track if you make a wrong career decision.

Use this chapter whenever you are thinking seriously about promotion. Use it to help you to focus on the activities you need to undertake to enable you to progress. Use it to help you to focus your attention on what you need to do next, and to help you to judge if what you are doing now is right for your career.

If you have already gained promotion, use this chapter both to evaluate your success to date and to help you to decide where to take your career next.

You will find the activities on motivation and on setting career goals in Chapter Two, and the activities on producing and implementing your career action plan in Chapter Four, useful in helping you to prepare to work through this chapter. If you have not completed these activities, you can still use this chapter now to help you to take stock of your situation, to assess the opportunities available to you and to review your current approach to managing your career.

The chapter is divided into four further parts:

- climbing the ladder
- making the right choices

- thinking about headship
- damage limitation.

Use the questions in the chapter as well as the answers offered to help you to decide on your next career move and to evaluate the success of your career management strategy to date.

5.2   Climbing the ladder

If you are thinking about promotion, you are almost certainly thinking about making your way up a career hierarchy and looking to gain greater rewards and more recognition as a result of taking on posts with more responsibility.

Yes, I've decided I really want to advance my career, so how do I start?
Now is the time to think seriously about the options for advancement and the opportunities available to you.

If you are looking for promotion, you need to do more than think about what you like doing, what you do well and what you would like to do more of. These things are important, but if promotion is your aim, you must also think about the availability of promoted posts, and how well your areas of interest, achievement and specialism are rewarded.

Read the educational press and visit relevant websites. Look at all the job adverts, not just the ones that are relevant to you. Do an analysis of what is available and which types of promoted posts are advertised most often. Note the specialisms where there are most opportunities for advancement. Note also how geography affects the situation. Are there more opportunities in one part of the country than in others? Are there opportunities abroad which interest you?

Seeking promotion will require you to develop a long-term career management strategy. You will need to analyse the market over time and watch for trends. Remember to look for developments and emerging opportunities in the state sector, in the independent sector, in the field of education management and possibly abroad. Then think about how you intend to shape your career to enable you to take advantage of the opportunities you find. This may mean that you need more training. It may mean that you need more experience.

By completing this type of review – and repeating it from time to time – you will be more aware of the state of the education market. This is vital information. You cannot manage your career effectively without it.

What are my options for promotion?
Organizations, including schools, normally organize their promoted posts into line management and functional responsibilities.

Those holding leadership roles have formal authority covering the management and delivery of a school's programmes and services. Managers and leaders have authority over people, too. Head teachers, deputy heads and assistant head teachers, heads of department and pastoral heads of house or year all have formal line management responsibility in school.

Teachers looking to progress via academic routes will usually seek to become a head of department, for example, head of mathematics or head of geography. Thereafter, they may progress to become a head of faculty where they have over-arching responsibilities for a number of smaller departments, for example, becoming head of modern languages or head of humanities. Teachers choosing the pastoral route usually become a head of year or a head of house.

Functional responsibilities are often specialist roles. They are usually advisory roles taken up by experts in precisely defined fields. Functional managers offer expert guidance to those with line management responsibilities. The experts in assessment, special educational needs and continuous professional development are all examples of people holding functional responsibilities. While line managers have formal authority, they will often defer to their colleagues with expert knowledge in their specific fields.

If you are considering academic and pastoral development routes, these are the progression routes which usually take you towards whole school leadership roles. Those who hold functional roles, and who seek to progress further up the hierarchy, will find that they usually have to take on a line management responsibility in order to do so.

The higher up the school hierarchy you go, the more likely you are to hold responsibilities which combine line management and functional responsibilities and which have a whole school focus.

There are also progression routes within education, but outside schools. Local authorities operate education departments, and people working there in advisory functions have usually held posts in schools first. You may decide you wish to develop your career in education management, working either in a local education authority or in government agencies. You might also wish to consider working abroad either in the short term or for a longer period of time. You may decide to think about exchanges or about working in schools which deliver the British curriculum or about if you could deliver another country's own curriculum. Your choices depend on what you want from your career.

There is also the inspectorate. This development route may be of interest to you as you progress into more senior roles. If you think becoming an inspector might be the right development for you, as well as finding out the entry requirements, talk to those who work as full-time and as part-time inspectors.

If you are not based in the United Kingdom, you should consider these development options with reference to your own education system. What are the opportunities for promotion in the government-funded education sector and in the private education sector? If you considered working abroad, where might you want to work, and which of your skills would be most highly valued in a different education system?

It is at this stage in your career that you begin to realize the value of having career aspirations and career goals. There are so many opportunities out there that you need to think carefully about which ones to pursue.

People tell me promotion is difficult. Are they right?
It depends.

There are lots of different ways to manage a career and ease or difficulty in gaining promotion depends on a range of variables. One of the most important factors to take into account is the relationship between the supply of teachers with particular skills and qualifications and the demand for that expertise.

There are often shortages in some areas and an over-supply of teachers in others. In broad terms, teachers of maths and science are more likely to be in short supply than are teachers of the humanities, liberal arts or the most popular media-related subjects. When thinking about the demand for teachers there are always more opportunities for promotion in core curriculum subjects than there are in subjects which only some schools deliver or which are offered only to a limited number of learners. Therefore, whether promotion is easy or difficult will be affected by what you actually teach.

Also affecting the ease or difficulty with which you will gain promotion is the way in which you manage your career. Some people will be more successful than others in both finding promotion opportunities and making sure they are able to take them up. Some people are more committed to the task of gaining promotion than others and some people will try harder to gain promotion than will others.

When people tell you that promotion is difficult, make sure you know if those offering their opinions have taken the time to analyse the market and then to develop their expertise, over time, to enable them to apply for the sorts of posts of responsibility that are advertised, because all of these actions make a difference to promotion prospects.

Job titles can be deceptive. How will I know if a post I am thinking about applying for is really a promotion?
Most people use the quoted salary to help them to answer this question, although this will not always lead to the right answer. You might earn less in a very senior role in a small school than you would earn in a less senior role in a large one. In such a case, if your key success criterion is the salary, then you might favour one role. If making your way up the hierarchy is your objective, you could favour the other.

If you want to be clear about how senior a post really is, work out how close to the top of the organization the role is. If you take on the responsibility, will you report directly to the head teacher? Will you report to someone who reports to the head? Will you report to someone else? The closer you are to the head teacher in terms of accountability, the more senior the post, however the job is described.

Might I have to go back to college and retrain if I am serious about getting on in teaching?
You should try to avoid this.

Whatever your subject specialism, or starting point, if you are committed to gaining promotion, there are ways of moving forward. There are, for example, cross-school responsibilities, including liaison with the local community, subjects such as citizenship, and all aspects of personal and social education that you can take on or train, part time, to undertake.

Even if you work in a subject area with limited opportunities for promotion, you can find ways of progressing your career by broadening your expertise and looking for promotion beyond your specialism. You may choose to take on pastoral responsibilities. There are also functional responsibilities, such as continuous professional development (CPD), that you can learn about, if you wish to broaden your skills and hence to develop your chances of gaining promotion. There are additional qualifications you could study in many, many disciplines, the majority of which can be studied part-time, that will help you to advance your career.

If you know where you want to go, you will begin to find ways to make progress towards your destination.

What else can I do to advance my career?
Associating with the right people is a good choice of activity.

Ask yourself who you know who holds the sort of role that you are looking to gain. This is a useful activity because one way of learning more about a role is to spend a day or more shadowing a person who is in the post. This means, quite literally, following the person around as he or she works. Becoming that person's shadow.

Job-shadowing is accepted as an effective approach to CPD these days, so you may find your school is supportive of a request to shadow someone. Just make sure the person you want to shadow understands what you are hoping to gain from the activity, and agrees to your request. Explain that you are shadowing him or her because you want to develop an understanding of the scope and breadth of that person's role, and to understand what it is like to work in that specific job. Be clear about how the shadowing activity will help you to fulfil your career action plan before you ask to shadow someone.

If you are thinking about very different sorts of roles from the one you hold at present, or which are available in your school, you still need to find people doing the job and talk to them. Look around. Are there conferences that these people attend? There are, for example, conferences on assessment, new qualifications, early years education, CPD and so on. If you attend, try to find out about the problems people working in those roles face, and how they deal with them.

Are there magazines and other publications linked to the role or the family of roles you are interested in? Are there websites and discussion forums for the people in the jobs you aspire to hold? Visit the websites. Find out if outsiders, or those aspiring to become involved in this area of work, are permitted to join the forums. If you can, join and learn. Make a point of finding out about the realities of the role and thinking about how your experience is preparing you to succeed in that sort of job. You can start with both of these activities right now.

Getting on in teaching is really important to me. Should I ever take a job I know I won't like, just to get me a bit further up the career ladder?
This is not a question anyone else can answer for you. In the end this sort of choice is one for you to make. Before you make it, however, you should think about the benefits, the risks and the 'what if' questions which surround such a career move.

The first question is: are you sure you need to make this move? Is this move one that is so important to your career management strategy that you believe you need to make it? Could you gain the experience you are hoping this job will give you in some other role, one that you will enjoy more?

You are probably thinking about moving into a job and staying there for only a limited period of time, maybe a couple of years. How do you know you will be able to move on at the end of two years? How do you know the experience you will gain in this role will be the sort of experience that will enhance your career? What if you find you can't move on as you had planned and what if the experience you gain is not quite what you expected?

Don't just think about the ramifications of taking on this type of role in the context of your working life. What will be the impact of taking on a role that you do not find satisfying and fulfilling on your personal life? How will the job affect your relationships? If the job entails a move to a new area of the country, will you be able to afford property in that area? Will you be able to sell your house both when you are moving to the new job and when moving on from it?

In other words how sure are you that your plans will work out as you expect? Weigh up all the options before you make your decision about this job.

5.3   Making the right choices

Once you have begun to take your approach to career management seriously and to plan your career systematically, your real job is to ensure you make the right choices when you are looking to advance your career.

Is there one right way, or a best way, to manage a teaching career? No, there isn't.

Just as there are different concepts of what constitutes a career there are lots of different, and equally sound, ways of managing your career. What is best for you will depend to a very great extent on what you want to achieve, which takes you back to your career aspirations and career goals and to your motivation (see Chapter Two). You might be aiming to get to any number of different places – and different types of promotion – so there have to be different ways of getting there.

Don't just think in terms of career development strategy leading to headship. When you are planning your strategy, at the very least think about:

- the level of reward you are looking for
- the type of work that will give you satisfaction
- the extent to which you wish to compete with other teachers for promoted posts.

Considering these three elements will help you to manage your career in the way that best suits you. For example, you can think about the salary levels you are looking for, and stop climbing the career ladder when you get there. You can also think about the type of work you find satisfying, or rewarding, in a more personal sense and seek that out.

You can think about how competitive you want to be. Getting to the top in teaching is very competitive. The higher you go, the greater the rewards and the responsibilities, but also the more intense the competition. Make sure you know how competitive you want to be.

If there isn't an accepted way of managing a career, how can I be sure that I'm making the right choices?

There are several things you can do to help you with this question. The first is to be clear that when you define the 'right choices', you are thinking in terms of what is right for you. To help you to do this, think about the differences between success and achievement.

As a teacher you are achieving things all the time. As someone who is committed to making progress with your career and gaining promotion, you will have a long list of achievements to your credit. Some of these you will draw attention to when you are applying for jobs and presenting yourself to a prospective employer. However, the most important question to consider is not what you have achieved, but how much value you place on your achievements.

Do you value your achievements? What you have done may amaze others, but if you do not see such achievements as anything special, you will not call it a success. The difference between your achievements and your successes is the value you place on them. Your successes satisfy and fulfil you; they will make you think well of yourself and be proud of your actions.

You will be making the choices that are right for you when you are pursuing roles that will help you to achieve, but which will also enable you to be a success, as you define it. When you are successful, in this context, you are making the choices that are right for you and choosing the right promoted posts, those which will also give you satisfaction and a sense of enhanced self-worth.

I've been teaching a long time and made good progress, but I've never set any career goals. Should I bother now?

If you're happy with where you have ended up, then you can feel satisfied with what you have achieved. However, it sounds as if luck has played a part in your success, which really turns the question back onto you. Ask yourself this question: are you happy to trust the rest of your career management process to luck?

If you decide you want to adopt a different approach, you can do so at any time. It's up to you to work out how much you think you would gain from planning your career. If you're ready to start planning, try to set yourself some career goals. Think about how you want to manage the next five years of your career and where you would like to be in your career at the end of those five years.

5.4   Thinking about headship

Every teacher interested in promotion must, at some point, consider whether headship is the right career goal. This choice is central to the definition of a teacher's career management strategy.

How soon must I decide whether or not I want to be a head teacher?
You should decide as soon as you are comfortable about making the decision. It will inevitably affect your career management strategy for the foreseeable future and it will shape all your career management plans.

Making this decision will have two immediate results. First, it will help you to be clear about the development path you will take. If you decide you wish to become a head teacher, you will be pursuing a linear career path with a defined destination at the top of the school career hierarchy. Second, your decision will close off a range of other development routes which do not lead to headship.

What will be different about my development path if I decide I want to become a head?
Deciding to become a head means you have made a clear and unambiguous choice to seek out the most senior leadership role in a school. This decision has ramifications for your whole career management strategy.

The definition of leadership in education is broadening all the time. If you want to become a head, these days, you are aiming to do more than become a leader of an educational community. You are looking at a general management role which encompasses responsibility for the major functions you find in a business: human resources, finance, marketing, operations, etc., as well as maintaining overall responsibility for the teaching and learning process and for the welfare and well-being of the learners in school. To a very great extent you will become the public face of your school when you become a head teacher, so you must expect to be in the spotlight as well as working hard behind the scenes to make your school a success.

What this means in terms of your career management process is that whenever you have a choice you are likely to be opting for whole school roles, and roles which help you to develop a strategic perspective on education. You will also need to understand something of how the different functions in school operate and gain experience of working in a number of them.

You will almost certainly need to gain line management responsibility. This means having responsibility for the quality of other people's work, possibly leading a large department in school, or a key stage. Sometimes, it is possible to progress a long way via functional responsibilities, including advisory roles, such as whole school responsibilities for CPD or assessment. However, holding line management responsibility is also necessary if you are looking for promotion to the most senior posts.

As you consider each new role, think about how this career move will take you closer to your destination of headship.

Is a higher degree essential if I want to become a head?
There is a trend towards more people taking higher degrees during their careers to help them to get ahead. The sort of higher degrees these people choose are those linked to the areas in which they want to gain promotion.

If you want to be a head teacher, then you may find it helpful to hold a higher degree. If you wish to work in an education department in a local authority, you may also find it useful. Whether a higher degree is essential is a grey area. You should find out if those people who are becoming heads in your area tend to have higher degrees. Look at job advertisements and read the person specifications linked to headships. Is a higher degree essential? Is it desirable? Do the adverts specify in which specialisms the higher degrees should be?

There are also professional qualifications for head teachers and for those aspiring to be head teachers that you need to consider. In some cases you will be expected to complete these programmes either before, or immediately after, becoming a head. Check out what is happening where you work and with people who have recently travelled along the same career path. Have they completed both types of qualifications?

Then make a judgement about the benefits you are likely to gain from undertaking extensive extra study. Ask yourself, and keep on asking yourself, how will the programme you are considering advance your career? Will achieving a new qualification take you closer to becoming a head teacher?

Will I need a coach or a mentor to help me to develop myself to become a head?
You need to be clear about the differences between coaching and mentoring before you make a decision.

Coaching is becoming a popular means of developing people, particularly senior people, in their posts. A coach will aim to help you to meet the challenges you face in your role and focus on solutions which are specific to you. He or she will support and encourage you along the way, but will also offer criticism where necessary. Think about sports coaches to get a better understanding of a coaching relationship.

Coaching is often offered to senior people by their employers and there has been a growth in this sort of coaching, often known as executive coaching, in education in recent years. It is most often made available to head teachers, but it is sometimes offered to deputy head teachers and assistant heads, too.

In many cases the coach has held a senior role in education and is someone who has faced similar challenges to the ones you are facing. Thus, he or she can give you insights into ways of dealing with leadership issues. Coaches can also help to facilitate your own development to enable you to find different and more successful ways of dealing with the issues you face at work.

Your mentor, whose focus is on supporting you, as an individual, and on helping you to fulfil your aspirations and to reach your goals, will have a broader perspective. Your mentor will help you to see your current role within the context of your whole career and your mentor will think about more than helping you to success in your current role. You will almost certainly choose your own mentor who may, or may not, be from education.

Once you are clear about the differences between coaching and mentoring, you can decide if you intend to seek out support in either field and how you will benefit from such support.

What do I do once I've made it and become a head?
When you have finished celebrating, you will need to start all over again with your career planning, but it will be a different sort of planning this time.

For a while your career management strategy will be all about finding answers to a range of questions which include:

- What do I want to achieve as a head?
- How am I going to judge if I am a success?
- Will I be looking at more than one headship in the course of my career?
- How long do I wish to remain a head teacher?
- What sort of a professional support network do I need to develop now I have become a head?

It's worth spending some time establishing aspirations and goals for the next stage of your career, because there are lots of head teachers who lose focus and direction in terms of their career management strategy once they take up their first headship. You are in as much danger of drifting after you become a head as you are at any other stage in your career.

5.5   Damage limitation

Careers do not always progress smoothly or in the directions people plan. Plans can go awry. Sometimes a lack of planning means that teachers end up at the wrong career destination, and in places where they are very unhappy. In such cases you will need to do your best to minimize the impact on your career.

The school where I work recently received a terrible inspection report. How can I stop this from damaging my career?
The first thing you must do is to try to look at the situation rationally.

Consider how much responsibility for the poor inspection results you bear. If you currently hold a relatively junior post, or if you have been in your post for only a short period of time, the inspection result may not really reflect badly on you. If this describes your situation, and you have decided you want to move to another school, just apply in the normal way. Look for the jobs that will help you to fulfil your career goals and career action plan. Don't allude to the inspection results in your application. Don't apologize for them. If the issue is raised at interview, describe your role and your involvement in the inspection honestly.

If you were responsible for an area that fared badly in the inspection, or if you had held a senior position in the school for some time before the inspection, then you will need to be clear about the lessons you have learned from the experience of inspection. You will need to be able to explain how the poor results have led you to change your practice and improve your performance.

In some cases, if you are determined to move on quickly from the school which received the poor report, you may need to consider a sideways move to find a new job. On the other hand, you may decide to stay, meet the challenges of improvement, and demonstrate that you can succeed in a school which has faced, and overcome, problems. Whatever choice you make, be sure that you understand the reasons behind the actions you take.

I've stayed in my current role for too long. Do I stand a chance of getting a promotion now?
Who says you have been in your current role for too long?

How long is the right amount of time to be in a job? There is no single right answer. There are lots of reasons why people stay in their jobs just as there are many reasons why they move on. You might have stayed because you have been working on a long project. You might have found the job changed underneath you while you have been in post, so in reality you have held several different positions without changing your job title. You might have your own reasons for having stayed where you are, reasons which have nothing to do with your work. Perhaps your personal circumstances have changed now and you are ready to think about promotion.

Think positively. Think about the benefits you have gained from being in your post for a substantial period rather than focusing exclusively on any problems your choices may have created. Think about what you can offer now you are thinking of moving on and what a different school will gain by employing you. Don't underestimate yourself.

Am I too old to become a head?
It's a good question. There is a lot of interest in age-related issues at present and people's attitudes to age are changing.

Think about your own attitude to your age first. Do you believe there is a right time in your career to become a head teacher? Do *you* think you're too old to become a head? Do *you* think it's too late for you to take on this role? These are relevant questions.

Your beliefs and attitudes matter. Even if you make applications for headships and obtain interviews, if you don't believe you stand a chance of getting the job, then you probably won't present yourself well. In such a situation, you might not be seen as the best candidate, so you will be unlikely to get the job. Thus, your belief about your inability to gain a headship will be reinforced.

Taking this line of thought a little more broadly, there are now laws aimed to prevent people from being discriminated against on the grounds of their age. This means employers should no longer be using age as a selection criterion. If employers are expected to stop thinking about whether someone is too old or too young for a role, shouldn't you follow suit?

I think I'm being held back by my lack of qualifications. What can I do?
On the surface this seems to be a very simple issue. If you think you need extra qualifications, then the answer is to find a way to gain them.

This may mean studying part-time, or it may mean taking some time out of your job, possibly without pay, to gain the qualification you need. You will know how important the qualification is with reference to your long-term career aspirations, so you can assess how big a sacrifice you need to make to gain the award you think you lack.

However, it's also worth asking your colleagues, and people in your professional support (see Chapter Four), if the qualification you are thinking about is an absolute necessity to enable you to fulfil your career goals, before you make any commitments to study.

Try to put your situation into perspective. If your concerns are linked to your entry qualifications into teaching, you may find that your experience and your successes in school since you became a teacher make up for the initial perceived shortcomings. If you are thinking about a promotion, are there routes, other than those linked to additional qualifications, that can take you to the right career destination? As ever, talk to the people in the roles to which you aspire about their journey and about their experience and qualifications.

Be honest with yourself, too. Are you saying the lack of qualifications is holding you back when perhaps there may be another reason? Do you really want to move on, or seek promotion? Do you want an excuse to stay as you are? Do you think you ought to be moving on, but are reluctant to do so? Allow yourself to look into your concerns and to reflect on your judgements.

Summary

1. This chapter is for teachers seeking to progress their careers by gaining promotion.
2. It can be used by teachers at all stages in their careers and wherever they are in the educational career hierarchy.
3. Teachers considering promotion should first become aware of the range of opportunities that exist and review these opportunities in terms of line management and functional management progression opportunities.
4. Whether teachers will find promotion easy or difficult depends on a range of issues including the demand for the individual's area of specialism, the numbers of teachers looking for promoted posts and the individual teacher's commitment to progress his or her career.
5. When thinking about promotion, teachers may need to extend their skills and broaden their experience in order to succeed.
6. Teachers should learn as much as possible about the types of promoted posts in which they are interested, and seek out those who already hold those posts in order to confirm their understanding of what specific jobs require of role holders.
7. There is no single right way to manage a teaching career.

8. Sound career management practice will lead teachers to seek out roles which give them satisfaction as well as delivering status and rewards.
9. Teachers are recommended to decide as soon as is practicable if they wish to progress to headship. This decision will have an impact on teachers' career management strategies.
10. Those seeking headship will look for whole school responsibilities and leadership responsibilities wherever possible and for continuous professional development opportunities which extend their abilities in these areas.
11. Once a teacher becomes a head, the career planning process begins again.
12. When teachers believe they have made career mistakes, for example, staying in a post for too long or lacking the qualifications they need to progress further, they should check that such perceptions are valid before taking action.

Activities

The activities linked to this chapter will help you to analyse systematically the opportunities for promotion which you identify. They will also help you to be clear about where posts you may be interested in sit in the educational hierarchy and to plan your own journey towards promotion.

Activity one – Knowing what's out there

Overview

This activity will help you to analyse the detail of opportunities for promotion in teaching and decide if those opportunities are appropriate for you. You can use the approach set out here whether you are looking for your first promotion or for promotion leading to more senior posts.

Whenever you identify a post that you think you might wish to apply for, complete this activity.

The activity is in two parts. Choose the part which is more relevant to your situation.

Part one – Climbing the ladder
Use the guidance here to help you to investigate the appropriateness of available promoted posts. Use the table on page 97 if you are interested in gaining your first promotion. Use the table on page 98 when you are looking for promotion to more senior posts.

1. Copy the table from page 97 or 98 and complete it with reference to each job you are interested in applying for.
2. Keep your notes related to each post safe and review them from time to time. Look for trends and check that you have acted on any feedback you have received at any point in the application process.

Part two – Planning your own career
Adapt the information in the two tables to help you to plan your own search for the right promoted post more effectively.

Job title (First promoted post)

Job role	Academic	Pastoral	Functicnal	Other
(tick as many as apply)				
Advertised where (journal, website, etc.)			Advertised when	
Salary				
Status – reports to someone 1, 2, 3 moves from the head teacher				
Why you are interested in this post				
Location – local, house move not needed – implications for you				
Location – house move needed – implications for you				
Issues about your career aspirations and goals highlighted by your interest in this role				
If you are successful in your application, what will be your likely next career move?				
Outcome – application/ interview, etc.				

Job title (Senior responsibility)				
Job role	Whole school responsibility	Line management responsibility	Functional management responsibility	Other responsibility
(Tick as many as apply)				
Advertised where (journal, website, etc.)			Advertised when	
Salary				
Status – reports to head teacher/someone else				
Why you are interested in this post				
Opportunities for your development in post				
What experience does this post require?				
What qualifications does this post require?				
Actions you still need to take in order to be ready to apply for this type of post				
Location – local, house move not needed – implications for you				
Location – house move needed – implications for you				
Issues about your career aspirations and goals highlighted by your interest in this role				
If you are successful in your application, what will be your likely next career move?				
Outcome – application/interview, etc				

Activity two – Aiming higher

Overview

This activity will help you to identify progression routes to posts with greater responsibility. It is in two parts. Part one deals with a case study. Part two deals with your own career.

Task

Read the following information about Mitch. Then consider the questions which follow. Record your responses on a piece of paper and keep your notes safe.

Part one – Mitch's career plan

Mitch is a teacher of science. He has been in teaching for four years and knows that he wants to become a head of subject, and possibly a head of science. He trained in chemistry and he has developed an interest in environmental science. He also knows that at some point in the future he wants to write a textbook about science teaching. He has taken on responsibility recently for curriculum development and helps the new teachers in the department to find their feet.

Using your own experience as a teacher to help you, and what you have seen about how people progress their careers in schools where you have worked, consider how Mitch will need to answer the following questions if he is going to fulfil his career goal: to become a head of subject or head of science and his career aspiration; to write a text book about science teaching.

1. How many career moves will it take me to get to where I want to be? *(Map them out.)*
2. What sort of roles will I need to take on before I achieve my goal? *(Make a list.)*
3. What additional experience do I need to enable me to reach my goal? *(Itemize the types of experience.)*

4. What sort of timetable for reaching my goal should I set myself? *(Draw up the timetable.)*
5. What types of professional development will I need? *(What sort of training and other development is needed?)*
6. Will I need a higher degree or something similar? *(Make a judgement about this or seek advice.)*
7. What are the next actions I need to take if I am going to get where I want to be? *(What is the first thing to be done to move nearer to the goal?)*
8. What could get in the way of my achieving my ambitions? *(What are the main issues to be considered in professional life and in life outside work?)*
9. Will I do better in a bigger school, or in a smaller school? *(Rate the advantages and disadvantages of both.)*
10. How should I judge my success? *(Think about something tangible – gaining a post, succeeding in a post, etc.)*

Reflecting on Mitch's career

- Is there anything else that Mitch should take into account as he plans his route to promotion?
- At which point in his development do you think Mitch will be ready to write a textbook?
- What should Mitch do to ensure he does not lose sight of his aspiration to write a textbook?

Part two – Your own career

Complete the following in the context of your own career.

1. Identify a goal you have set yourself that leads to promotion.
2. Consider the ten questions above and write down your answers with reference to the goal you have set yourself.
3. Ask yourself: is there anything else you should take into account as you plan your progress up the career hierarchy?
4. Revise your notes and keep them safe.

5. Review your notes, and update them as appropriate, as you work towards your goals.

Notes – About Mitch's career development

Provided you have encouraged Mitch to be clear on the differences between being a head of subject, for example, chemistry or environmental science, and the role of being a head of science, which is a more senior leadership role, where Mitch will have responsibility for disciplines other than his own, and for the work of more people, you have probably offered some good advice.

Mitch almost certainly needs some more experience in teaching and in a broader range of roles before he can think about writing his textbook. Knowing this could be a useful insight for him.

Refer to the notes you have made when completing these activities whenever you are thinking about seeking promotion.

Chapter Six

Changing direction

6.1 Overview

This chapter is for teachers reconsidering where they want to take their careers and for teachers who are not sure if they want to pursue the career plan or path they have been following.

Wherever you are in your career right now this chapter will help you to decide how to manage the next stage in your career journey, especially if you know you do not want to seek promotion.

It will help you to be more aware of what you find satisfying about your work and what you might wish to aim for in teaching if you are not looking for promotion. Finally, it will help you to assess, or to re-assess, your understanding of what constitutes a successful career and to review if you are pursuing the right career management strategy for you.

Use this chapter whenever you think it is time to look closely at your career management strategy and whenever you are considering making major changes to your life as a teacher. Work through this chapter to help you to find the right next career step for you.

Use this chapter in conjunction with Chapters Two, Four and Five.

The chapter is divided into three further parts:

- ever upward or not
- changing gear
- re-assessing what's important.

You will find questions that teachers reviewing the ways in which they manage their careers often ask themselves under each of these headings. Review the answers to the questions as you work through the chapter and judge how relevant they are to your circumstances.

6.2   Ever upward or not

Every teacher, at some point, considers whether to go all out for promotion or to manage his or her teaching career differently. If you decide not to pursue promotion, you still have a career to manage.

I don't want to go after promotion. Does that mean I'm a failure?
No.

It's an old-fashioned concept of a career to think in terms of always moving up a career hierarchy, taking a different job every couple of years in order to progress, and climbing to the top of the career ladder. This was never reality for the vast majority of teachers. Only one person in a school can be the head teacher at any one time, and only a small proportion of teachers will ever become head teachers. If every one is aiming to get to the top, to gain a headship, then most people are going to be disappointed.

You are not a failure for not wanting to seek promotion. If you plan your career carefully, if you are clear about what you want to do with your career, if you have a plan to help you to get to the right destination for you, and you then arrive at that destination, you are successful.

Remember different people are motivated in different ways and want different things from their careers. See Chapter Two for guidance on this. What is important is knowing how you need to manage your career to make sure you succeed in the terms that you define success.

I've been offered a promotion. Can I afford to turn it down?
Whether the role you have been offered brings a promotion

with it or not is not the issue. It's more important for you to consider if this is the right job for you. Whatever you want from your teaching career, will taking this job help you to move closer to reaching your career goals?

If there is something about the job that makes you uneasy, or makes you reluctant to take it on, will a higher salary or enhanced status compensate for your lack of enthusiasm for the post? If it will, then you are likely to accept it. If it won't, you are likely to turn the post down. If you feel guilty for even thinking about turning down a promotion, have you allowed an assumption that every one 'should' be looking to get to the top to influence you? Are you thinking about accepting the post because other people tell you it is the right thing for you to do?

If I don't want promotion, does that mean I'm stuck in the job I'm in now for the rest of my life?
No, it doesn't.

You are in charge of your career, so you decide when you want to change your job. The best time to look for a new job is when you believe a change of post will help you to achieve the career goals you have set yourself. This may mean you look to change your job when you want to do something different in teaching, or to live somewhere else, when you develop expertise that you cannot use in your current role, but would like to, or when your personal circumstances change. Sometimes you will need to be proactive about change. Sometimes exciting opportunities will present themselves to you. Remember it's your choice how you proceed towards the goals you have set yourself.

If I'm not looking for promotion, what should I be looking for in my next job?
Having decided you are not looking for promotion allows you to view your career differently. You can now think about pursuing your interests and developing your talents without worrying about finding a way to climb the career ladder, too. Look to find ways to help you to fulfil your career action

plan, to achieve your career goals and to help you to feel satisfied with your working life.

If you are not pursuing promotion, then you are likely to be considering one or more of the following when you start to look for your next job.

The type of role you want – you may have developed expertise in a new area and are looking for a post that allows you to use your new skills. You may be looking for a different mix of responsibilities. You may be looking for a complete change.

The level at which you wish to work – you may know the level in a school at which you are most comfortable. Are you happiest as a team member, or as the leader of a small team, or in a specialist role? You may have gained promotion but know you do not wish to progress any further up the career hierarchy. Therefore, you may also consider sideways moves, to enable you to develop your expertise and your interests without necessarily taking on more senior responsibilities.

The type of environment in which you wish to work – you may be working in a large school at the moment and are looking to work in a smaller organization. You may be looking to work in a different phase of education, moving from secondary to primary or into further education. You may be considering moving into the independent sector, or from the independent sector into the state sector. You may be interested in working in a specialist school or in an academy. You may be looking to work in a rural school, or an urban school, or a school that is facing challenges.

The organizational culture that best suits your working style – you may be looking for a school that is more go-ahead, or more traditional, or more business-orientated. You may be looking for a school that uses different teaching methods from those favoured in your current school, or one which adopts particular approaches to dealing with behaviour management issues. You may be looking for more or less formality in the management or leadership style.

6.3 Changing gear

Sometimes changing career direction can also mean slowing down. It can mean taking on roles with less responsibility. It can mean reshaping your career and your approach to career management quite radically.

I hold a post of responsibility which I no longer want. Can I give it up and just teach again?
There are no rules which say you can't do this, but it is an unusual move, and one you need to think about very carefully before taking action.

Think about yourself, first. How would you deal with being in a junior position again, and having to follow the instructions of other people, some of whom you might, at some point, find yourself in disagreement with? You would no longer have the status in school which will allow you to follow your own path. Note that the further up the hierarchy you have progressed the harder you are likely to find relinquishing status.

There is also the issue of salary. You will almost certainly earn less if you take on a post with less responsibility. Have you thought about this? You need to think about your life-style and your financial commitments, but you must also consider the impact such a move would have on your pension. The older you are, the longer you have been in teaching, and the nearer you are to retirement, the greater the likely financial impact of such a decision. This is an instance where you would be well advised to take professional advice about the financial implications of the career options you are considering, sooner rather than later.

Do people really move down the career ladder through choice?
They do.

Not all changes that take you down the career ladder, rather than up it, are forced on people. Sometimes they simply choose to manage their lives in different ways. This way of managing a career is often called downshifting, and downshifting is becoming more widely accepted in the workplace today.

Don't be certain that your colleagues and your senior team will necessarily be that surprised if you decide to give up some of your responsibility. Downshifting can be a very attractive option. Downshifting occurs when you decide to stop chasing promotion and being work-driven and to rethink the way you organize your working life. It is about changing the pace of your life, especially your working life, changing gear, in fact.

If you are seriously considering this as a career option, before you give up your responsibilities, you may wish to discuss the concept of a responsibility break with your head teacher or with your governors. A responsibility break will give you a breather from the pressures of your current promoted post and give you a chance to rethink your career plans.

Alternatively you might decide to take a career break. This is quite literally taking time out from your job, without pay, to give you the opportunity to deal with issues in other parts of your life, or just to allow yourself the space you need to plan and to think. This may, in itself, sound like a radical move, but if it helps you to make the right decision, you may think it is worth it.

Will people still take me seriously if I give up my seniority?
In the end what other people think is their concern. None of us can force people to think in particular ways, nor to hold particular opinions about us. They come to their own decisions, just as you do.

You can try to influence people, but there are limits to anyone's influence. Bearing this in mind, ask yourself just how important other people's judgements are to you. Does it really matter what others think, or don't think about you? It's your decision.

There are things I have to do at home that mean I can't keep up with my responsibilities at school. Will I have to resign?
Resigning would be the final step, the step you would take if

every strategy you use to reconcile the demands of home and work on your time fail. It should not be your first thought, especially if you enjoy teaching and are reluctant to give it up.

Ask yourself, first, if what you have to do at home is a long-term or short-term commitment. If your partner has suffered a stroke or a heart attack, for example, then you will hope that the extra stress and extra load you are carrying now will diminish as your loved one's health improves. Thus, you may only need to seek to rearrange your responsibilities for a relatively short period, say six months or a year. You may be able to negotiate some changes in your school life with your head teacher that will help you to get through this difficult time without needing to think about resigning.

If your home commitments have increased significantly and, as far as you can judge, are unlikely to diminish again in the foreseeable future, you will need to think about the implications of this change in the context of your working life and with respect to all aspects of your life outside work. In this case you may be considering making decisions that will affect your whole life – now and for the future. You may also be considering making these decisions in stressful circumstances. Since these changes are far-reaching, consider calling on the support of your networks, both your professional support network and your personal support network, to help you to work through the issues. See Chapter Four for information about support networks.

Consider also part-time working options, and relinquishing responsibilities and promoted posts before you decide you have no alternative but to resign.

Can people who are not teachers help when I am thinking about making radical changes to my teaching career?
People outside education face many of the same challenges that teachers face and must deal with the universal career management and life management decisions, just like you. These include making decisions about jobs, about

relationships, about retirement, about moving house to take up a new role and so on.

Of course, there's nothing quite like the pressures of being a teacher, but you're not talking to members of your personal support network who are not teachers about your teaching role. On this occasion you are talking to them about career management and life management issues. Thus, they may have some valuable support to offer. Moreover, you may be talking to people who know you well. In some cases they will have known you for much longer than you have been a teacher. Their views may be helpful to you and they may offer insights which those who only know you in a professional context cannot.

If I'm making changes to how I manage my life outside work, might these changes affect the way I manage my career, too?
They might.

You will have created an unrealistic career management strategy and action plan if you have articulated career aspirations and set career goals without thinking about your plan in the context of your whole life, because creating a plan with just your working life in mind will usually cause problems sooner or later.

Don't think of your career as totally separate from the rest of your life. Consider the changes you make to how you manage your career, as a result of reviewing your aspirations outside work, as part of the process of making your career action plan more realistic and more achievable.

6.4   Reassessing what's important

If you decide you are not looking for promotion, or if you want to change gear or change direction, this may lead to your reconsidering your whole approach to how you manage your career.

I've achieved a lot in my teaching career, but it doesn't mean very much to me any more. What's the matter with me?
Are you sure anything is the matter with you?

If what you have achieved meant something to you in the past, but you no longer place as much value on it, you need to think about what has changed. Why do you value what you are doing less now than you once did?

If your school still values your achievements, but you do not, perhaps you should look at your own approach to judging your success. It may be that you have a tendency not to value anything you do once it is no longer a challenge for you. If this is the case, recognize that achievement for you is found in overcoming difficulties, not in completing a task, or doing something well. Perhaps you should remind yourself that doing things well, even when the challenge in the task has gone, is still an achievement and something to be proud of.

If other people still place a high value on what you do, then it seems likely that your judgements about what is satisfying and fulfilling about your work are changing. This means it is time to do some hard thinking about your career goals, and your career aspirations, too.

I used to enjoy working at the weekends, but now I resent the extra time I spend on school work. How can I justify making changes to how I work? My job still needs to be done.
The answer here is all to do with the ways in which you define work. When you really enjoyed what you were doing, although it was technically labelled work, in your case, what you did at the weekends was probably a recreational activity for you.

This is often the case with professional people. They want to spend more time thinking about their specialism than their working hours demand. While you're enjoying what you do, you see no problem with putting in those extra hours. After all, you are choosing how to spend your own time.

Yet, when something changes, and you no longer view that extra time spent on your work as enjoyment, you think differently about how you use your time. You suddenly resent giving extra hours to your job.

Ask yourself what activities your work is now displacing. How would you rather be spending the time? If you are unhappy with your current situation, how can you cut down your work commitment? Ask yourself what would happen if you halved the extra hours you are giving to your work? Consider also if there are ways in which you could reallocate your time at work to allow you to complete the tasks you now do at home in school. Could you relinquish any of the tasks you currently do? Are you doing some things which are not part of your job, or which could be done more efficiently by someone else?

Remember that by asking yourself these questions you are aiming to create more time for yourself in your life outside work, which you can then use in ways you find more satisfying.

I have a career action plan, but I don't want to complete it. What should I do?
Never force yourself to work on a career action plan that is no longer right for you. Review your plan and rewrite it if necessary.

As you take a long look at your plan, work out whether there are just parts of it that you no longer want to complete, or if you are dissatisfied with the whole thing. Note how long it is since you last revised and updated your plan. Have you neglected it? Have you outgrown it?

Once you review your action plan, don't criticize yourself for changing your mind. It's perfectly reasonable that your career aspirations should change as you progress in your career. If you have been a teacher for a number of years, then you will inevitably rethink some of your career aspirations and career goals as a result of being more experienced. Your life experience will also affect your career decisions. This is why you can only plan so far ahead, maybe two career moves, maybe five years into the future.

The problem that many teachers face is that they don't recognize when their aspirations are changing, or when what's important to them is changing. For example, at some points in your life your career is very important to you. At other points life outside work takes precedence. There are no rights and wrongs about this and no 'shoulds' and 'oughts'. What's important is that you become aware of how your goals and aspirations are changing and then act on this knowledge.

The mistake many teachers make is to continue to pursue a career management strategy which no longer has relevance to them and which no longer fires them with enthusiasm. Check out if this is true in your case.

What sorts of things could make me change my career management strategy?
There are lots of things that can affect your approach to how you manage your working life. It would be impossible to set out an inclusive list. Some of the most common reasons why people change direction, or to think differently about their careers, are linked to their lives outside work. These include:
changes in relationships – changes that lead to loved ones demanding more of you as an individual or new relationships that make different demands of you. These changes can affect your approach to how you manage your career.
births and deaths – the birth of a child will affect your working life as well as your home life. This might encourage you to reassess how you manage your career. The death of a loved one can be the catalyst that leads you to rethink any number of aspects of your life.
illness – personal illness, or the illness of others who are close to you, can put additional pressures on you. You may need to take on a caring role yourself. Through ill-health you may need to limit your commitment to your work and you might require someone to care for you, either for a short period or for a more extended period.
life experience – we are all the sum of our experiences. Your experiences will shape your beliefs, what you value, what you want to do with your life.
age – we all view life differently as we age. We also have different commitments at different points in our lives. Our

personal circumstances change. We may be more or less
affluent. We may think very differently in our forties from
how we thought when we were younger. When we approach
our sixties we could have very different views from those we
held thirty years previously.

Be aware that what happens in your life outside work
directly affects your life as a teacher and take this into
account when you are planning your career and when you
are reviewing your plans.

Summary

1. This chapter is for teachers who are reconsidering
   where to take their careers.
2. It will help teachers to decide how best to manage
   their careers if they are not seeking promotion. It will
   also help teachers to be more aware of what they find
   satisfying about their work and how to assess if they are
   pursuing a career management strategy which is right
   for them.
3. Teachers who decide they do not want promotion still
   have a career to manage and need to think about the
   roles they wish to take on, the level of responsibility
   they are most comfortable with, the types of environ-
   ments in which they wish to work and the culture of
   organizations they are considering working in.
4. Downshifting, or giving up the work-driven lifestyle,
   is becoming more widely accepted in modern
   workplaces.
5. Teachers thinking of relinquishing responsibilities
   should consider how willing they are to give up salary
   and status, and how these career choices will affect
   their pensions, before taking action.
6. Teachers taking on additional responsibilities outside
   teaching, including caring responsibilities, should
   explore options for part-time working, the reduction
   of responsibilities and career breaks before resigning
   their posts, especially if they enjoy teaching.

7. Teachers are recommended to call on the support of their professional support network and their personal support network when thinking about major changes to the ways in which they manage their careers.

8. Factors influencing teachers' choices about the ways in which they manage their careers include: changes in relationships, births and deaths, illness, life experience and age.

Activities

The two activities linked to the content of this chapter will help you to decide what sort of career you wish to pursue, if you are considering changing direction. The first activity will help you to be more aware of why you are considering this change. The second activity focuses on the type of role you arc likely to find most satisfying.

Activity one – Time to change?

Overview

This activity will help you to work out what is prompting you to think about changing career direction.

Task

1. Look at the statements which follow and write down on a sheet of paper the letters of the statements you agree with.

   I am thinking about changing direction because:

   A. I want more time for my hobbies and interests outside school.

   B. I don't get on with the senior people in school.

   C. I no longer enjoy my job.

   D. I want a job where I can use more of my skills.

   E. I want a job where my talents will be appreciated more.

F. My job is no longer challenging.
G. I am finding my job more and more difficult.
H. I want to work in a different field in education.
I. I want a job where I can be more creative.
J. I dread going to work each day.
K. I need more time to study.
L. I want to get away from the squabbling and politicking in school.
M. I want to learn about different aspects of teaching.
N. I want to do more interesting work.
O. I want a job where I have more freedom of action.
P. We all have so much work to do in school that I dislike working there.

2. Review your notes. How many of the following have you chosen?
    B, C, F, G, J, L, P.

The more of these items there are on your list, the more you are thinking about getting away from your current role than you are thinking about what you want to do instead of continuing in your current job. Use this knowledge to help you to answer the remaining questions.

3. Where you have chosen any of the specified responses (B, C, F, etc.) answer the questions below which relate to your responses. Allow yourself sufficient time to consider how the changes you are considering would affect your life as a teacher and make a note of your answers.

    • I don't get on with the senior people in school, but if I did, what difference would that make to me and to my work?

    • I no longer enjoy my job, but if I did, what difference would that make to me and to my work?

    • My job is no longer challenging, but if it were, what difference would that make to me and to my work?

    • I am finding my job more and more difficult, but if I did not, what difference would that make to me and to my work?

- I dread going to work each day, but if I did not, what difference would that make to me and to my work?
- I want to get away from the squabbling and politicking in school. If I could, what difference would that make to me and to my work?
- We all have much so much work to do in school, but if we did not, what difference would that make to me and to my work?

4. Now look at the remaining items on the original list (items A to P) that you have selected. Consider the questions below which relate to your responses, and make a note of your answers.

- I want more time for my hobbies and interests outside school. What specific changes do you intend to make to enable you to have this time?
- I want a job where I can use more of my skills. Which of your skills do you want to use more? What do you need to do to ensure you are able to do so?
- I want a job where my talents will be appreciated more. Which specific talents do you want to be appreciated more? What can you do to make certain they are?
- I want to work in a different field in education. In which field specifically do you wish to work? How do you intend to get there?
- I want a job where I can be more creative. What specifically do you mean by being more creative? What changes can you make to the way in which you work to enable you to have more opportunities to be creative?
- I need more time to study. How much more time do you need? How do you intend to reorganize your life to enable you to find the time you are looking for?
- I want to learn about different aspects of teaching. Which aspects of teaching do you want to learn

about? How do you intend to manage this learning process?

- I want to do more interesting work. How do you define interesting work? What do you intend to do to ensure your work is more interesting?
- I want a job where I have more freedom of action. Specifically, what sort of freedom are you looking for? How do you think you can obtain this?

5. Now review what you have written. How many of the objectives you have specified do you think you can meet while in your current role?

6. What do all your responses tell you about:
    - why you want to change direction
    - what sort of role you are looking for?

Record your judgements and keep your replies safe.

Activity two – Making the right move

Overview

Since you are not seeking promotion, you do not need to think about making your way up a career hierarchy or climbing the career ladder. You should, however, think about what motivates you in your career.

Task

To help you to manage your career and your career moves effectively, think about:

- the type of **role** you are looking for
- the **level** in school at which you wish to work
- the type of **working environment** you are looking for
- the type of **organizational culture** in which you wish to work.

1. Re-read the part of the chapter which deals with these issues then, on a separate sheet of paper, note three

things you will be looking for with respect to each of these characteristics:

- role
- level
- environment
- organizational culture.

2. Note down your answers to the questions which follow and keep your responses safe.
    a. How similar are your preferences to your current experience of a career in education?
    b. If you decide to try to shape your career to match your preferences, what career goals will you now identify? (How will you manage the next two career moves, or the journey towards the role you wish to hold in five years' time?)
    c. How will these new goals affect your existing career action plan?
    d. What changes to your career action plan will you need to make to accommodate all your goals?
    e. What could get in the way of your achieving your goals?
    f. What is the next activity you intend to complete to take you nearer to achieving your career goals?

Refer to the notes you have made when completing these activities whenever you are reassessing your approach to how you manage your career.

Chapter Seven

Leaving teaching

7.1 Overview

Every one leaves teaching sooner or later, but some teachers don't wait until retirement to do so.

This chapter is for teachers who are asking themselves if the time is approaching when they will leave teaching, possibly for good.

Teachers leave teaching for lots of different reasons. Some teachers decide they don't like the job. Some find it too difficult or too stressful a role. Some decide there are other things they want to do more than they want to teach.

Sometimes this career choice will be about whether to change direction or whether to think about leaving teaching. Therefore, read this chapter in conjunction with Chapter Six.

Use this chapter to help you to be clear on the issues you need to consider if you are thinking about whether you should stay in teaching or leave. Use it to help you to clarify your thoughts and to ensure you ask yourself relevant questions about the choice you are thinking of making.

The chapter is divided into two further parts:

- changing horses
- thinking about retirement.

You will find questions that teachers thinking about leaving teaching often ask themselves under each of these headings. Review the answers to the questions as you work through the chapter and judge how relevant they are to your circumstances.

7.2   Changing horses

At any point in your career you might think about leaving
teaching, following a different career path and defining new
career goals. You need to understand why you are considering such a decision, and to take some time before you
make your decisions to ensure you understand your motivations and the consequences of your proposed career
choices.

*I don't know anyone who has left teaching other than to retire. Am I
unusual in thinking about leaving?*
No, it's more common than you might think.

In any profession or career people join the workforce but,
for whatever reason, choose not to stay. Teaching is no
different from other occupations. You will find that
approaching half of those who begin their training to
become a teacher have left the profession before they have
completed three years as a teacher.

There's also something of an hiatus when people have
been teaching for seven or eight years. By this time they
understand the educational system, the nature of the career
opportunities available to them and how progression and
promotion work. Those who leave sometimes do so because
they do not wish to climb the career ladder. Sometimes they
leave because they cannot see the sort of future they are
looking for in teaching. In most cases teachers themselves
make these decisions.

Other reasons why people leave are related to issues such
as ill-health, changes in their personal circumstances and so
on. These are exactly the same reasons why a proportion of
people leave any occupation.

Don't think you're on your own in considering leaving
teaching. You're not.

*I'm starting to think that teaching really isn't for me. How can I be
sure? I don't want to make the wrong decision.*
You're right to want to analyse your situation before you
take action.

Your next step depends a lot on how long you have been in teaching. If you have only been a teacher for a short period – say less than a year – look at Chapter Three.

If you have been a teacher for some time, ask yourself if you have just started to doubt whether you want to stay in teaching, or if the feeling has been growing for some time. Is this change in your view of teaching related to a specific incident at work or to something that is happening in your life outside work? Why are you thinking about leaving teaching rather than changing direction or looking for a different sort of job? Use Chapter Six to help you to answer these questions.

If you believe that your change of heart about teaching has occurred gradually, over time, try to think when the change started and what could reverse it.

In all cases, try to work out why leaving teaching appears to be a better option than moving within the profession or staying where you are.

Are there good reasons for leaving teaching?
There are and, for the most part, you decide whether your reasons for leaving are good or not.

Good reasons for leaving will include those where you are moving for positive reasons. If you know that however much you enjoy teaching you are leaving to do something you will enjoy even more, that is a positive reason for leaving. Knowing why you are moving on is always a good idea. Being able to articulate your reason is even better.

If you believe you are doing the right thing by leaving teaching and, after planning carefully, and discussing your plans with people in your support networks, and listening to their responses, you feel the same, you may have found some good reasons for leaving.

Isn't it a failure to leave teaching before retirement?
Failure is a strong word and it suggests you see a decision to leave teaching as a defeat of some sort.

You need to be more aware of how people manage their careers these days. People are less likely to enter a career in their twenties and stay there throughout their working lives than they once were. People move from job to job more often and from occupation to occupation. Teachers are no exception.

People also take more responsibility for their own careers today including taking responsibility for sustaining their employability, that is, their ability to hold down a job. There is also a lot of interest in skills updating and in transferable skills. There is more of an expectation on the part of people in employment to be able to move from one career to another without need to retrain completely these days.

All the people who move from one career to another are not failures, but they are choosing to manage their working lives in different ways from those which were more common in the past.

How, exactly, do I leave? What should I do?

It's never a good idea to march through a career door and slam it behind you, so do your best to part with your school on good terms.

Make sure your head teacher and your governing body know why you are leaving. Try to communicate a positive message. Acknowledge that teaching is an excellent profession, but there are reasons why it is no longer for you.

Ask for testimonials. These are written statements about you which someone writes at your request. Testimonials make statements about you and what you have done in school. They may talk about your character or about your achievements. Approach several senior staff in your school for testimonials which demonstrate different achievements. Also check that you can approach more than one senior person in school for a reference, now or in the future.

Make sure you understand and follow the rules in your contract of employment for resignations and notice periods. Talk to someone in your employing organization – your local education authority, for example – about your pension. Speak to the human resources people about the procedures for ending your employment. If you are going to a new job, they will need to know to whom they should send information about your employment. If you are not going into another job, you will want the papers associated with the end of your employment sent to you.

Do everything you can to part with as many people as possible on good terms. Do your best to keep doors open. You might want to come back into teaching at some point, and you want to present a professional and conscientious image right to the end.

What do people who leave teaching do?
Almost everything.

Some go into other jobs. Some start businesses. Quite a lot of ex-teachers seek out roles where they can use the skills they have developed in teaching, for example, work that involves making presentations. Some choose to go into careers linked to their subject specialism. Some retrain entirely. Some move into other industries, but which serve the educational sector. Educational recruitment is one example of this. You will also find ex-teachers working in companies which sell specialist products and services to the education sector.

Some teachers know exactly where they are going when they leave teaching. Others take some time to find the right career for them.

7.3   Thinking about retirement

The whole subject of retirement has become a major issue for teachers in recent years. People are living longer. Retirement ages are rising or disappearing altogether in some countries. As a consequence, retirement, pensions and related issues are likely to remain in the news for some time.

What do I need to know about retirement before I get there?
The most important thing to know about retirement is that it is about change. It's about a big, big change.

When you retire you move out of the world of teaching into a very different world. You are exchanging a salary for a pension. You are leaving your school community. You are leaving behind the responsibilities you held. You will have time on your hands, unless you plan how you are going to manage your life. This means thinking about financial issues, working out how much money you are going to have in retirement and what you intend to do with it. It also means thinking about how to keep healthy and how to make sure you are able to enjoy life once you leave your job in school.

There are lots of organizations offering advice to people about to retire or who are within five years of retirement. If you use your preferred internet search engine to locate them, you will see there are significant numbers to choose from. Their strongest and most consistent message is that you should plan carefully and make sure you know how you are going to organize – and also fill – your life once you have retired.

I want to enjoy life more now. School is so overwhelming and so exhausting, I think I need to find a way to retire as soon as possible. What do I do?
There's no reason to wait until you retire to live the life you want to lead.

If school is taking too much out of you, maybe you need to think about looking for a job with less responsibility or perhaps you should look into working part time. See Chapter Six, which is about changing direction, but also consider the implications of any career choices you make on your pension.

Work out what you want from life and then think about how you can find ways of achieving your aspirations now, or in the near future. Then look at whether seeking retirement is the right choice.

Is retirement the end of my working life?
That's very much your own choice.

People who work after retirement, and there are growing numbers of people who are doing just that, often do so for different reasons from the ones that took them to work when they were younger. Work creates a social environment that people want to be part of. Work helps to keep people active and engaged with life in their community. Work has a social element, too. For some people there are also financial reasons why they continue to work. For example, they may have debts that they need to pay off or they may wish to sustain a lifestyle that cannot be supported by their pension alone.

For all these reasons people carry on working after they retire. You may decide to carry on working, too. Whether you come back into teaching or undertake some other type of work is all about personal choice.

Summary

1. This chapter is for teachers who are considering leaving teaching.
2. The chapter will help teachers to ensure they ask themselves relevant questions as they consider whether or not to leave teaching.
3. Teachers leave teaching for different reasons and they leave to do lots of different things.
4. It is more common these days for people to move from occupation to occupation during the course of their working lives. Teaching is no exception.
5. Teachers most often leave when they have been teachers for only a short period, although they may leave when they decide they do not wish to make their way up the educational career hierarchy.
6. It is best to leave teaching for a positive reason: to do something that a teacher likes even more than teaching.
7. Teachers considering leaving teaching should consult specialist advisers before making their decision. They should also try to remain on good terms with people in school.

8. Teachers who are retiring need to be aware of the magnitude of the change they will be making when they leave.
9. Growing numbers of people continue to work beyond retirement today. Many teachers do this, too.

Activities

The two activities linked to the content of this chapter will help you to think carefully about your preparations for leaving teaching. The first activity deals with the decision to leave teaching when you are not thinking about retirement. The second focuses on the issues you will need to consider as you approach retirement.

Activity one – Making the big decision

Overview

This activity focuses on why you might want to leave teaching and how you will communicate your intentions to the most important people in your working life and in your life outside work. Completing the activity will help you to be clear about why you are thinking seriously about leaving teaching.

Task

If you have begun to think that leaving teaching is the right career move for you, how might you explain your decision to the important people in your working life and in your life outside work?

1. On a separate piece of paper make a list of who you will need to tell about your decision. The list is likely to include:
   • family members
   • your closest friends

- your colleagues
- your manager (e.g. head of department or head of year)
- your head teacher.

Add to this list if you think there are any omissions.

2. Take each person or group of people on your list in turn and note down how you will explain to each of them:
   - why you are thinking about leaving teaching
   - why you think this will be the right career choice for you
   - why now is the right time for you to make this decision.

3. Review your responses and summarize your statements under the headings in question two above. Note the differences between what you say to the different groups of people.

4. Now think about your career in teaching and note down your responses to the questions below.
   - If you leave teaching, what will you miss?
   - If you leave teaching, what will you be glad to leave behind?
   - Have you any plans about what you will do once you have left teaching?

Activity two – Thinking about retirement

Overview

This activity focuses on some of the issues you will need to think about when you are trying to decide on the right time to retire from teaching.

Task

1. On a separate sheet of paper note down what you think would be good and bad about retiring at each of the following ages:
   - before you are 60

- 60
- 63
- 65
- 67
- 70
- after you are 70.

2. Review your answers and make sure you have considered:

- financial issues – your ability to finance the lifestyle you want to lead in retirement
- pensions issues – your understanding of the size of pension you will receive if you retire at that age and how well its buying power is likely to be sustained through your retirement years
- skills and experience – your willingness to stop using your skills, experience and knowledge at that age
- health issues – your judgement about your ability to continue to work after that age
- social issues – your judgement about how leaving work would affect your friendships and other social relationships
- family and close relationships – your judgement about how leaving work would affect your relationships with members of your family and those with whom you have close personal relationships.

3. Make a judgement about the best age for you to retire. Note this down along with at least three reasons why you think this age would be the right one for you to choose.

4. Now investigate the feasibility of your analyses. Take advice from a number of sources as you do so. Then discuss your proposals with senior people in school and with people in your life outside work who are important to you.

5. Create an action plan leading to your retirement which takes into account your own aspirations, the advice you have received from various sources and the requirements of your employing organization.

6. If you are thinking about taking on different work once you have retired from teaching, complete the activity again as appropriate.

Keep your notes safe and refer to them whenever you are thinking about your departure from teaching.

Chapter Eight

Putting it all together

8.1   Overview

This chapter is for teachers looking to draw together the career planning lessons they have learned as a result of working through part, or all, of this book.

Use this chapter to help you to create, to refine and to update your career management plan. Use it to signpost you to the guidance in different parts of the book and to the various activities which will help you to improve your planning skills. Use it also to check that any career management plan you have devised using methods not covered in this book addresses all the relevant career planning issues.

Use this chapter at any point in your career and whenever you want to focus on your overall approach to taking charge of your teaching career.

The chapter is divided into three further parts:

- creating a career management plan
- developing your career planning abilities
- the final analysis.

You will find questions that teachers thinking about how best to plan their careers often ask themselves under these headings. Review the answers as you work through the chapter and judge how relevant they are to your circumstances.

8.2   Creating a career management plan

So far this book has helped you with the individual elements of the career management process. The main elements of this are:

- defining a context for your career development and understanding what motivates you
- establishing career aspirations and career goals
- producing an action plan and an associated implementation strategy
- establishing a contingency plan
- creating a means of reviewing your career planning from time to time.

If you are going to be confident that you really are in charge of your teaching career, you will need an overall career management plan which brings together all these elements. You will create that plan either as a result of undertaking the activities in this book or as a result of completing some other career planning process which you value.

What does a good career management plan look like?
That can be quite difficult to establish.

Career management plans come in different forms and formats so it's not always easy to decide if a planning process or planning template is any good. However, a good career management plan will be made up of several important components. Refer to Appendix One for a list of the main elements that you need to include in your plan.

If you are using an approach different from the one in this book, make sure that all the elements noted in Appendix One are represented in your plan. A good career management plan will, at the very least, cover all these issues.

How should I use the activities in this book to help me produce a career management plan?
First of all you should complete the activities which are

relevant to the career management decisions you are working on right now.

The activities at the end of each chapter focus on the key elements raised in that chapter, and the decisions you are likely to be considering, if you have chosen to read the chapter. Completing the activities will help you to think more deeply about the issues you are working on. For example, the activity at the end of Chapter One, entitled 'Looking ahead', will help you to look three years into the future, rather than simply thinking about finding the next job. That activity helps you to begin to think about career goals and possibly about career aspirations. The first activity at the end of Chapter Four, entitled 'Building your support networks', helps you with the concept of resourcing your career plan and finding the right people to help you to make your career management process more robust.

The main reason you have been asked to make notes about each activity, and to keep your notes safe, is to ensure you have some background information to support you as you begin to create an overall career management plan. If you look at Appendix Three, you will see how the activities in the book are linked to different aspects of the career planning process.

Should I produce a single document to capture all the career planning elements in one place?
You should consider doing so, as having a single document will help you to see what you are planning and what you intend to do to achieve your career goals. If you date your document, and also project forward to a time when you intend to review your plan, it will help you to keep track of what you are trying to achieve and if you are succeeding in what you are trying to do.

Also, if you keep printed copies of your plan rather than simply updating your intentions on your computer, you will be able to chart your progress as time passes.

I want to be systematic about career planning, so what does the career planning process look like?
If you decide you want to see an overview of the whole process then Figure 8.1 will help. In Figure 8.1 the main career activities are set out as a linear process.

Figure 8.1: Principal career planning activities

However, you will not always plan in quite so linear a fashion.

Sometimes, for example, it takes a while to decide on goals. In the meanwhile you still have day-to-day decisions to make about your career. It can also take time to get feedback from your professional support network or from your personal support network about what you are planning. This might mean you proceed to other aspects of the planning process while you are waiting to hear from these people.

Therefore, remember that you will have to be flexible in your approach to how you plan. Use Figure 8.1 as a guide rather than an instruction on how to proceed.

How will I know that the career plan I produce is sound?
That's easy in retrospect. If you adhere to your plan, and if it helps you to manage your career in the way that is right for you, then you will know you have a good plan. However, if you want to assess the value of your plan along the way, you will need to think about how you use it.

Is your plan something you refer to regularly and use to guide your day-to-day decisions about how you manage your career? If it is, and if you find the plan helps you to make decisions you are happy with, then the chances are your plan is sound.

If, on the other hand, once you have completed your plan, you put it away and don't look at again it until it's time for your annual review or when you are thinking about applying for a job, your plan is unlikely to reflect your real aspirations and goals. If, in this situation, when you look at your plan, you find some surprises and statements that you no longer agree with, then your plan is probably not very sound. This will mean it needs revision.

Another good way of testing the quality of your planning is to talk through the detail with someone whose judgement you respect and who is willing to spend time helping you to plan and to manage your career. As often as not, you will see the major flaws in your planning process as discuss your plans with someone who has an interest in helping you to manage your career.

Are there particular times when I should ensure I make use of my career management plan?
Yes, whenever you reach, or your think you are approaching, one of the major decision points in your life, or in your teaching career.

These are the points at which you make far-reaching decisions: accepting a promotion, turning down a promotion, prioritizing an aspect of your life outside school over your career, switching specialisms or deciding to specialize in one area, deciding to leave teaching, etc.

At these times – all of which can be stressful times – having a plan which you have prepared over time and which you have prepared with the help of people whose judgement you value and respect, will be very helpful in your decision-making process.

What's the most important thing for me to remember once I have my career management plan in place?
The plan belongs to you.

It is your plan and your responsibility both to implement and to keep up to date. If you find your plan no longer reflects what you want to do with your teaching career, then repeat the planning process and update your plan.

If you have successfully completed the actions in your plan, set some more goals. Look further ahead in your career.

If you are still working on your plan, and you are still working towards the goals you have identified, even after the deadlines you set have passed, check that your career management strategy is still realistic. Revise your plan as necessary.

If you are struggling with the planning process, think about the expertise you need to plan more effectively.

8.3 Developing your career planning abilities

People do not simply plan well without practice. Planning is a skill and it takes time and effort to develop that skill. Think about the expertise you need to produce an effective career management plan and take steps to make sure you develop your planning abilities.

What are the most important career planning abilities?
There are lots of important aspects of career planning but there are two which are probably more important than any others. These are the ability to think clearly and the ability to be honest with yourself about how you are progressing with any plan you produce.

Clear thinking is an essential element of planning. On this occasion you are planning your own career, so no one else will be in a position to think as clearly about this as you are. You need to focus on the task and to understand what you are trying to achieve.

Being honest with yourself is also important. If you are not achieving the goals you have set yourself, you need to know why. You need to know if you have just not applied yourself. You need to know if you want to achieve those goals. Have you put down what you really want out of your career in your plan, or have you written down what looks right or what you think you ought to have in a plan? Are you sure you will be content if you achieve the goals you have set yourself? Are you allowing yourself to progress your career in the way that is right for you?

What's the most important judgement I need to make when I am planning my career?
When you have completed your career management plan, you will almost certainly have your own views on the answer to this question.

However, one of the most important judgements you must make is the one that helps you to be certain that the goals you have set for yourself are goals that will give you some satisfaction to reach. You need to be certain that you are climbing the right mountain and putting your efforts into tasks that will give you satisfaction when you complete them. Gaining a headship is not a success if, along the way, you have discovered that you really don't want to be a head teacher after all.

What can I do to make sure I am focusing on the right things?
A good way of doing this is learning to ask yourself the right questions. Good questions help to clarify your thoughts. They also help you to focus on specific issues.

Whenever you are reviewing your career management strategy, ask yourself which are the six most important questions you should be considering at that time. You may find it helpful to link one question to your career aspirations, one to your career goals, one to your career action plan, one to how you are implementing your plan, one to how you are dealing with the problems and issues that might get in the way of your completing your plan, and make sure one is linked to how you review your success and plan for the next stage in your career.

Use the list of questions in this book to help you to choose the right questions for you. See Appendix Two for the complete list.

8.4   The final analysis

Will taking charge of my teaching career help me to achieve better work–life balance, too?
Almost certainly.

Work has the potential to dominate teachers' lives so getting control of work is an essential aspect of work–life balance. Getting control of your working life and preventing it from overwhelming the rest of your life is essential if you are going to achieve sound work–life balance. If you are in control of your working life, you are also making good progress towards achieving work–life balance.

Above all else what should I remember about this book?
You are trying to make sure you take charge of your teaching career, or remain in charge of it.

Once you have used this book to do so, use your success to date to build a working life that you will enjoy and one which meets your aspirations for fulfilment.

If you have developed these abilities, and use them, you will be on the road to success.

Good luck with your journey.

Summary

1. This chapter is for teachers looking to draw together all the career management lessons they have learned as a result of working through this book and to use their learning to help them to create a sound career management plan.
2. Career management plans can be presented in different formats but sound plans will include: career aspirations and career goals, a set of actions to be completed and an implementation strategy.
3. Resources to complete the activities in the plan, a timetable for action, a means of reviewing success and a contingency plan to help to put the overall plan back on track if problems with fulfilling it emerge are also needed.
4. Completing the activities in this book will help teachers to build up their abilities to formulate sound career management plans.
5. The teacher creating the plan owns the plan and is responsible for implementing it and for keeping it up to date.
6. In order to produce a sound career management plan teachers must develop good planning skills. The most important of these are the ability to think clearly and the ability to be honest with themselves about their progress with their plans.

7. In order to keep a career management action plan on track, it is helpful to keep asking oneself relevant questions. Choosing six from the list used in this book may be useful.

Activities

The two activities linked to this chapter will help you to review your overall approach to planning and managing your career. The first activity will help you to be sure the career management plan you have produced covers all the essential elements. The second activity will assist you to identify six key questions you will use to keep your career planning process on track.

Activity one – Your career planning checklist

Overview

This is a checklist activity to assist you in reviewing the completeness of your career management plan.

Task

Whatever approach you have chosen for career planning, use the checklist which follows to establish if your plan contains the following elements. Make a copy of the checklist and complete it.

Name	Date	Included in your plan
A review of this plan will be triggered by: *(defined event, a date, etc.)*		
Career Management Plan – this deals with what you intend to do		
1. Career aspirations – *(what you want to achieve, your over-arching aim)*		
2. Career goal or goals – *(a prioritized list – one, two or three manageable goals)*		
3. Your action plan – *(what you intend to do, set out in date order – in the next six months, one year, two years, five years, etc)*		
4. Your timetable for completion – *(ensure that all actions have a deadline, a date by which they are to be completed)*		
5. Resources – *(personal resource and external resource, include a list of people who will be approached for feedback and guidance)*		
6. Your implementation strategy – *(how you are going to make sure you fulfil your actions set out in 3 above – what specifically you will do)*		
7. Contingency plan – *(how you intend to get back on track if things go wrong, plus a list of possible 'what if' scenarios that you have considered)*		
8. Review of achievements – *(a review of activity and success in fulfilling your plan, including confirming that you have reached your goals and that you are satisfied with how you are managing your career)*		
9. Next steps – *(revisions to the plan, which will help you to address your career goals or to set new ones)*		

If you find your plan omits any of the above, consider how you intend to amend your planning process to take account of the issues you do not, at present, cover. You may include other, additional elements if you find them helpful.

Activity two – Six key questions

Overview

This activity will help you to identify six key questions to assist you in keeping your career management plan on track.

Task

1. Read through the list of career management questions used in this book which are set out in Appendix Two. Choose six that you believe are related to your current career planning priorities. Make a note of these questions. If you find it helpful, choose one question linked to each of the following headings:
   - career aspirations
   - career goals
   - your career action plan
   - your implementation strategy
   - your contingency plan
   - your means of reviewing success and planning the next stage of your career management journey.

2. As you undertake your career planning activities consider the questions you have selected, and the answers to those questions which are offered in the book. Then decide how you can use these answers to help you to manage your career more effectively. Make a note of your responses.

3. Update or construct a relevant career management plan.

Refer to the notes you have made when completing these activities whenever you are reviewing your overall career planning process.

Appendix One

Key elements of career management

This appendix sets out the key elements of the career management process. You will need to ensure you cover all these aspects of career management if you are going to be in charge of your own career.

Make sure your overall career management plan contains:

a context statement – explaining what has motivated you to draw up your plan at this particular point in your career.

career aspirations – which are your over-arching aims for your career, and the reasons for your career journey. They are what you want in the long term for your career.

career goals – the specific destinations at which you wish to arrive, for example, the specific posts or responsibilities you wish to hold as you work to fulfil your career aspirations. If you have more than one goal, then your goals should be prioritized.

your action plan/career action plan – the actions you intend to take to ensure you reach your goals, set out in a prioritized list. Your action plan will include statements about the resources you need to fulfil your plan and your timetable for action.

the resources you need to fulfil your plan – which include personal resources, such as the time and effort and sometimes the money you put into fulfilling your plan and the external resource, principally the guidance and advice you seek out from people whose judgements you trust.

your timetable for action – which indicates the estimates you have made of how long it will take you to fulfil your implementation plan and reach your goals or for how long you think your plan will be valid. Typically teachers can plan up to five years ahead or two career moves.

your implementation strategy – this sets out how you are going to make sure you complete the actions you have specified in your plan. It is a practical statement.

your contingency plan – a strategy for dealing with the things that can get in the way of your fulfilling your plan, a means of dealing with the unexpected and unanticipated or events which blow you off course.

a means of measuring your success – an approach for checking out how you are progressing with, and if you are achieving, your goals, an approach for confirming if you are adhering to your timetable and of checking how satisfied you are with how you are managing your career.

an approach for planning the next steps in your career – career planning is cyclic. As you achieve one set of goals, or as your circumstances change, your goals will need re-definition and your plan may need rewriting.

Appendix Two

Questions in the book

This appendix sets out all the questions from each chapter of the book.

Use this appendix to locate specific themes that are of interest to you and to focus on questions relevant to your current situation.

Chapter Two: Planning your career

2.2 Why career planning matters

- Planning is time-consuming and difficult. Is it really necessary?
- What is a career anyway?
- Is there a generally accepted definition of what a career actually is?
- This isn't the way I have heard careers described in the past, so are these other definitions wrong?
- I've got a definition of my career I'm happy to work with, so do I start to think about the jobs I would like to aim for?

2.3 Understanding yourself

- I don't really know what's important to me. What can I do to get started?
- How do I work out what motivates me as a teacher?
- It's not as simple as that. I'm motivated by more than one thing. What does that mean for my career planning?

- Should I also think about what motivates me in my life outside work?
- Once I've done that, am I ready to start to think about where I want to take my career?

2.4 Career planning basics

- Career goals and career aspirations. What are they, and what's the difference between them?
- I'm really struggling with this. Some people know where they want to take their careers. I don't. Does this mean I can't plan my career?
- How far ahead does this mean I should plan when I am thinking about my career goals?
- That's all very well, but so much happens that is unexpected in life, is it really worth spending all this time on thinking about career goals and aspirations?
- What happens if I want to change my career goals?
- I've got my aspirations and my goals, so can I think about the jobs I want to do?
- So what comes next in career planning?

Chapter Three: Starting your career

3.2 Starting out in teaching

- Every one seems to pay a lot of attention to induction and the induction process. Why is that?
- What should I expect of my induction?
- I only have my own experience to work with. How will I know if I am getting a good induction?
- When I get to the end of my first year in teaching, should I consider my induction has finished?

3.3 Survival strategies

- How am I going to get through my first term?
- What will my survival plan look like?

- What is the most important element of my plan?
- I can make more time for myself and avoid being overwhelmed if I cut out unnecessary meetings. Do I need to attend those sessions for new teachers in school and at the teachers' centre?
- How do I find the expert guidance I need to help me survive?
- Who else should I turn to for help?
- Every one tells me I've got a lot to learn. How do I find the time to act on all the recommendations about what I should do to improve my practice?
- Do I really need to read lots of books about teaching theory in my first year?
- Since I'm new to teaching, how am I going to avoid making lots of terrible mistakes?
- Teaching isn't for me. I know it isn't. What can I do?

3.4 Finding your very special talents

- It seems a silly question, but how will I know what I do well?
- How exactly can I use my progress reviews to help me to be aware of what I do well?
- There are lots of options open to me. Is it too early for me to start to specialize?
- How will I know what to ask to do more of next year?

Chapter Four: Developing your career

4.2 Establishing your development route

- There's such a lot I could do, where do I start?
- Do I need to think about specialization now?
- How can I make sure I am considering a broad enough range of development routes?
- Does thinking about the right development route mean that I will also need to think about continuous professional development (CPD)?

- How much CPD do I need?
- Will I need a higher degree?

4.3 Developing your career

- Do I really need career goals?
- What do I do once I have my career goals?
- I can see I need an action plan, but how will having an implementation strategy help me?
- What will go into my action plan?
- And what goes into my implementation strategy?
- Why is it important to include a timetable for action?
- What sort of resources do I need to fulfil my action plan?
- Who are the best people to help me to plan my career?
- How do I decide who should form part of my professional support network?
- How many people should I aim to bring into my support networks?
- What do I do if I get lots of different advice?
- That sounds complicated. Do I need to do all this?
- What do people get wrong when they plan their careers?
- What else could stop me completing all the actions I plan?
- If I think I'm now ready to produce an action plan and an implementation strategy, what do I do?
- How will I know when I am succeeding?

4.4 Finding the right school

- I thought I just looked for the job that is right for me. Why do I need to choose the schools carefully, too?
- How will I find the right sort of school for me?
- I know I want to move to a different part of the country. How can I investigate a school when I work a long way away from it?

- I'm worried about ending up in the sort of school where the workload will be enormous. How do I avoid this?
- How much should I take a school's reputation into account when trying to decide where I want to work?

Chapter Five: Seeking promotion

5.2 Climbing the ladder

- Yes, I've decided I really want to advance my career, so how do I start?
- What are my options for promotion?
- People tell me promotion is difficult. Are they right?
- Job titles can be deceptive. How will I know if a post I am thinking about applying for is really a promotion?
- Might I have to go back to college and retrain if I am serious about getting on in teaching?
- What else can I do to advance my career?
- Getting on in teaching is really important to me. Should I ever take a job I know I won't like, just to get me a bit further up the career ladder?

5.3 Making the right choices

- Is there one right way, or a best way, to manage a teaching career?
- If there isn't an accepted way of managing a career, how can I be sure I'm making the right choices?
- I've been teaching a long time and made good progress, but I've never set any career goals. Should I bother now?

5.4 Thinking about headship

- How soon must I decide whether or not I want to be a head teacher?

- What will be different about my development path if I decide I want to become a head?
- Is a higher degree essential if I want to become a head?
- Will I need a coach or a mentor to help me to develop myself to become a head?
- What do I do once I've made it and become a head?

5.5 Damage limitation

- The school where I work recently received a terrible inspection report. How can I stop this from damaging my career?
- I've stayed in my current role for too long. Do I stand a chance of getting a promotion now?
- Am I too old to become a head?
- I think I'm being held back by my lack of qualifications. What can I do?

Chapter Six: Changing direction

6.2 Ever upward or not

- I don't want to go after promotion. Does that mean I'm a failure?
- I've been offered a promotion. Can I afford to turn it down?
- If I don't want promotion, does that mean I'm stuck in the job I'm in now for the rest of my life?
- If I'm not looking for promotion, what should I be looking for in my next job?

6.3 Changing gear

- I hold a post of responsibility which I no longer want. Can I give it up and just teach again?
- Do people really move down the career ladder through choice?

- Will people still take me seriously if I give up my seniority?
- There are things I have to do at home that mean I can't keep up with my responsibilities at school. Will I have to resign?
- Can people who are not teachers help when I am thinking about making radical changes to my teaching career?
- If I'm making changes to how I manage my life outside work, might these changes affect the way I manage my career, too?

6.4 Reassessing what's important

- I've achieved a lot in my teaching career, but it doesn't mean very much to me any more. What's the matter with me?
- I used to enjoy working at the weekends, but now I resent the extra time I spend on school work. How can I justify making changes to how I work? My job still needs to be done.
- I have a career action plan, but I don't want to complete it. What should I do?
- What sorts of things could make me change my career management strategy?

Chapter Seven: Leaving teaching

7.2 Changing horses

- I don't know anyone who has left teaching other than to retire. Am I unusual in thinking about leaving?
- I'm starting to think that teaching really isn't for me. How can I be sure? I don't want to make the wrong decision.
- Are there good reasons for leaving teaching?
- Isn't it a failure to leave teaching before retirement?
- How, exactly, do I leave? What should I do?
- What do people who leave teaching do?

7.3 Thinking about retirement

- What do I need to know about retirement before I get there?
- I want to enjoy life more now. School is so overwhelming and so exhausting, I think I need to find a way to retire as soon as possible. What do I do?
- Is retirement the end of my working life?

Chapter Eight: Putting it all together

8.2 Creating a career management plan

- What does a good career management plan look like?
- How should I use the activities in this book to help me produce a career management plan?
- Should I produce a single document to capture all the career planning elements in one place?
- I want to be systematic about career planning, so what does the career planning process look like?
- How will I know that the career plan I produce is sound?
- Are there particular times when I should ensure I make use of my career management plan?
- What's the most important thing for me to remember once I have my career management plan in place?

8.3 Developing your career planning abilities

- What are the most important career planning abilities?
- What's the most important judgement I need to make when I am planning my career?
- What can I do to make sure I am focusing on the right things?

8.4 The final analysis

- Will taking charge of my teaching career help me to achieve better work–life balance, too?
- Above all else what should I remember about this book?

Activities in the book

This appendix will help you to be clear about how the activities at the end of each chapter are linked to the major stages in the career planning process.
These are:

- defining a context for your career development and understanding what motivates you
- establishing career aspirations and career goals
- producing an action plan and an associated implementation strategy
- establishing a contingency plan
- creating a means of reviewing your planning from time to time.

Complete the activities when you are working through the relevant chapter. Your answers will help you to deal with your immediate career planning concerns and to arrive at decisions about how best to develop or to refine your career management strategy.

Use the table on pages 158–9 to help you to decide which activities are most relevant to your circumstances and to your planning activities.

Guide to activities – How they help

Chapter	Activity	Linked to which aspect of the career planning process	Completing this activity will help you to …
One	Looking ahead	Establishing career aspirations and career goals	Be clear about what you want to achieve in your career in the next three years
Two	Motivation and you	Establishing career aspirations and career goals	Be clear about what motivates you in your career
Two	Career aspirations and career goals	Establishing career aspirations and career goals	Formulate career aspirations and career goals
Three	Creating your survival plan	Establishing an action plan (short term)	Produce a plan to help you to get through your first year in teaching, or your early weeks and months in a new job, with a degree of success
Three	Finding your very special talents	Establishing career goals and your action plan (short term)	Be aware of what you and others in school value about your contribution
Four	Building your support networks	Resourcing your career action plan and your implementation strategy	Identify a number of individuals who you would like to include in your support networks
Four	Defining an action plan	Producing your career action plan and your implementation strategy	Create or update a realistic career action plan and implementation strategy
Five	Knowing what's out there	Producing your implementation strategy	Produce an analysis of opportunities which are available to you or to which you can aspire
Five	Aiming higher	Producing your implementation strategy	Identify relevant career progressions routes

Six	Time to change?	Reassessing and reworking your career plan	Decide in which direction you wish to take your career, if you think the strategy you have adopted thus far needs revision
Six	Making the right move	Creating a new career management plan	Choose the right career progression route after revising your career goals
Seven	Making the big decision	Establishing aspirations for a career outside teaching	Be clear about why you are thinking about leaving teaching
Seven	Thinking about retirement	Considering the best time to retire Reviewing your planning	Be clear about the issues to be taken into consideration when you are thinking about retirement
Eight	Your career planning checklist	Producing an overall career management plan	Draw together all the components of a career management plan into a single document
Eight	Six key questions	Keeping your overall career management plan up to date	Be clear on your current career management priorities

Appendix Four

Further reading

Websites

Career management is a popular topic and there is no shortage of information in books, in journals, in periodicals and online about it. A good starting point for information about career management is the website of the Chartered Institute of Personnel and Development.
www.cipd.co.uk
There are lots of resources and fact sheets here, many of which can be accessed by those who are not members of the institute.

The websites belonging to teachers' unions and professional associations are useful resources for gaining an insight into the concerns of teachers and as a source of guidance on the main issues affecting teachers' careers.
   It is also helpful to look at websites which support teachers in more than one country to get a more complete picture of the range of career management issues which are of interest to teachers.
   In the United Kingdom the sites belonging to:
The Association of Teachers and Lecturers (ATL)
www.atl.org.uk
The National Association of Schoolmasters Union of Women Teachers (NASUWT)
www.nasuwt.org.uk
The Nation Union of Teachers (NUT)
www.teachers.org.uk
are useful sources of information.

Websites for senior staff in schools include those belonging to:
The National Association of Head Teachers
www.naht.org.uk
The Association of School and College Leaders:
www.ascl.org.uk
and The National College for School Leadership
www.ncsl.org.uk

Information about inspection and related issues can be found at:
www.ofsted.gov.uk

When considering sources of information about career management for teachers outside the United Kingdom, visiting websites belonging to teachers' unions and professional associations in relevant countries can be helpful.
The American Federation of Teachers' website
www.aft.org
gives a clear indication of the issues which are of most concern to teachers in the USA.
The Australian Education Union's website
www.aeufederal.org.au
and The New Zealand Educational Institute's website
www.nzei.org.nz
both help visitors to the sites to be more aware of the issues teachers in those countries wish to know more about.

Journals, newspapers and periodicals

The education world's journals, newspapers and periodicals are a source of valuable information about professional development, leadership, how teachers are dealing with particular career management situations, etc.
The Times Educational Supplement
www.tes.co.uk

Sec-Ed
www.sec-ed.com
are popular journals which cover all these issues. Both have extensive features archives.

Government agencies offer factual guidance on aspects of teaching, including qualifications, etc.
In the United Kingdom The Training and Development Agency for School (TDA) website:
www.tda.gov.uk
has sections for teachers, school leaders, support staff, etc, including guidance on continuous professional development (CPD).

Information on teachers' pensions is to be found at:
www.teacherspensions.co.uk

Books and articles

Work-Life Balance: A practical guide for teachers, Margaret Adams (2006), David Fulton Publishers.
'Don't leave the good times until you're sixty-five', Margaret Adams, *Times Educational Supplement,* 5 October 2005.
www.tes.co.uk
'Help! I'm in the wrong job', Margaret Adams, SecEd, 4 October 2007.
www.sec ed.com